WORSHIP CHANGES
Since the First Century

One of a Two-Book Series

**WANDERING SOUL,
ENTITLED HEART, AND
THE SIDE-TRACKED CHURCH**

By K. M. Haddad

Other Books by the Author

CHRISTIAN LIFE
Applied Christianity: Handbook 500 Good Works
You Can Be a Hero Alone
Worship Changes Since 1st Century + Worship 1sr Century Way
The Best of Alexander Campbell's Millennial Harbinger
Inside the Hearts of Bible Women-Reader+Audio+Leader
The Lord's Supper: 52 Readings with Prayers

BIBLE TEXTS
Revelation: A Love Letter From God
The Holy Spirit: 592 Verses Examined
Was Jesus God? (Why Evil)
365 Life-Changing Scriptures Day by Date
Love Letters of Jesus & His Bride, Ecclesia (Song of Solomon)
Christianity or Islam? The Contrast
The Road to Heaven

FUN BOOKS
Bible Puzzles, Bible Song Book, Bible Numbers

TOUCHING GOD SERIES
365 Golden Bible Thoughts: God's Heart to Yours
365 Pearls of Wisdom: God's Soul to Yours
365 Silver-Winged Prayers: Your Spirit to God's

SURVEY SERIES: EASY BIBLE WORKBOOKS
→Old Testament & New Testament Surveys
→Questions You Have Asked-Part I & II

HISTORICAL RESEARCH BIBLE
for Novel, Screenwriter, Documentary & Thesis Writers

HISTORICAL NOVELS & STORYBOOKS
Series of 8: They Met Jesus
Ongoing Series of 8: Intrepid Men of God
Mysteries of the Empire with Klaudius & Hektor
Christmas: They Rocked the Cradle that Rocked the World
Series of 8: A Child's Life of Christ
Series of 10: A Child's Bible Heroes
Series of 8: A Child's Bible Kids
Series of 10: A Child's Bible Ladies

Scripture taken from the New King James Version, Copyright @ 1982 by Thomas Nelson, Inc. Used by permission. All rights reserved.
Copyright © 2014 Katheryn Maddox Haddad
NORTHERN LIGHTS PUBLISHING HOUSE

ISBN 978-1-948462-90-7
Printed in the United States

In Praise of

WORSHIP CHANGES SINCE THE FIRST CENTURY

* * * * * LINDA R. ROBERTS.
I loved the book. A good read.

* * * * * VALERIE CARAOTTA. A comprehensive work depicting changes in congregational protocol and political structure

In Changes in Worship Since the First Century you will find a very comprehensive chronological account beginning with the first-century apostles and leading to our present day worship. It is not the "worship" in terms of singing but in terms of the structure of the early church and its changes. As you discover how Rome dominated the early church with the Catholic church emerging, it will be eye-opening how those that denied this faith's beliefs were tortured and killed-often burned at the stake. One individual, for example, was sentenced to execution for not going to mass, not making confession, and not believing the bread and wine was Jesus actual body and blood.

Author Haddad recalls how God's laws became lost in church legalism, rituals, and policies and actually resulted in more division among one another. She shares very candidly the following: "This is Satan's greatest weapon in the church. If he can build a hedge of creeds and regulations around an organization, it can choke out the primary purpose of the church's existence, and in the process choke out the church."

She encourages us to break away from traditional denominationalism and instead seek to unite with nondenominational brothers and sisters, adhering to the Bible only as the blueprint.

Church leaders and ministers will find the detail informative as a reference source and teaching aid. Individuals desiring to better understand church history will too find this a welcomed addition. Haddad has spent many years studying Biblical truths.

* * * * * JEWEL TAYLOR.
A very good book.

TABLE OF CONTENTS

Other Books by the Author ii
In Praise of WORSHIP CHANGES SINCE iii

IMPORTANT HISTORICAL EXPLANATION 1

1. CHANGES IN WORSHIP 1st to 12th Centuries
   1st Century 3
   2nd Century 4
   3rd Century 5
   4th Century 8
   5th Century 11
   6th Century 14
   7th Century 16
   8th Century 18
   9th Century 21
   10th Century 23
   11th Century 25
   12th Century 29

2. CHANGES IN WORSHIP 13th to 16th Centuries
   13th Century 35
   14th Century 37
   15th Century 40
   16th Century 49
   ENDNOTES 62
   BIBLIOGRAPHY 62

3. CHANGES IN WORSHIP 16th to 18th Centuries
   16th Century (cont) 64
   17th Century 75

4. NEW TESTAMENT-PATTERNED CHURCH
Europe 2nd – 15th Centuries 94
   2nd Century 96
   3rd Century 99
   4th Century 101
   5th Century 104
   6th Century 105
   7th Century 106
   8th Century 107
   9th Century 108
   10th Century 108
   11th Century 110
   12th Century 112
   13th Century 116
   14th Century 117
   15th Century 120
   ENDNOTES 127
   BIBLIOGRAPHY 128

5. NEW TESTAMENT-PATTERNED CHURCH
Europe 16th – 18th Centuries
   16th Century 130
   17th Century 142
   18th Century 149
   Conclusion 155
   BIBLIOGRAPHY 156

6. FORWARD! BACK TO THE FIRST CENTURY!
Divided We Fall!
   A chapter for our denominational friends 159
   Institutionalizing the Church 163
   Side-Tracking our Purpose 166
   Prejudice 169

Making Decisions for Us..171
Married to Our Institution..173
Power of the Individual..179
That They May Be One 181
Neither Catholic, Protestant, Nor Jew 183
Newness of Life...189

7. FORWARD! BACK TO THE FIRST CENTURY
United We Stand!..193
    Another chapter for our denominational friends..............193
    Re-educating our Consciences 197
    To Compromise..199
    The Secret: Conservative 204
    How Far is Too Far?..208
    ....Or Not to Compromise 210
    Back to the Bible 213
    A Personal Restoration Movement.....................................215
    Holy Wars 217
    Matters of Opinion..219
    Second-Generation Church Accounts 220
ENDNOTES...221

About Book II WORSHIP THE FIRST-CENTURY WAY 223

Thank You 224
Buy Your Next Book Now 225

Connect With The Author..226
Get A Free Book 226
Join My Dream Team 226

IMPORTANT HISTORICAL EXPLANATION

Before Separation of Church and State

To understand how only small protestant movements gained power one nation at a time despite the Holy Roman Empire (Catholic church) Headquartered in Rome, it must be understood that, since the beginning of time, every nation had its own special Guardian/Patron deity. The Egyptians did, the Babylonians did, the Hebrews did, and so on. Anyone who did not honor the government-selected deity could be imprisoned, tortured and killed — legally.

Constantine was the first emperor of the Holy Roman Empire to accept the God of the Christians as his official God. Thereafter, the Roman church had no problems using the empire's army to carry out its beliefs.

Eventually Martin Luther convinced the ruler of Germany, who did not like the pope, to declare his version of the Christian God as the official religion of Germany. Calvin convinced the Swiss government to declare his reformed version of the Christian God as the official religion of Switzerland. John Knox convinced the Scottish government to declare his presbyterian version of the Christian God as the official religion of Scotland. As so it went: As leaders of various countries broke away from the political and religious power of Rome, they declared yet a different version of the Christian God to be their official religion.

Despite this, there has always been a group somewhere organizing and worshipping the way the first-century church organized and worshipped. Though they tried to stay out of sight of their government, they were nearly always persecuted by both the Catholic church and the various protestant denominations founded by the above and other men. But God watched out for his own, and his church never died.

CHANGES IN WORSHIP ARE CENTERED

Commonly known hymns written by or for the persecuted are centered

Protests are in italics

Persecutions are in bold type

1. CHANGES IN WORSHIP

1st to 12th Centuries

1st Century

During the first century, the gospel was proclaimed by the Twelve Apostles and close associates everywhere: Philip in Phrygia, Turkey and Egypt; Matthew in Parthia, the near Orient, and Ethiopia in Africa; Andrew in Turkey and Russia; Mark in Egypt; Jude in Edessa, Parthia; Bartholomew in India; Thomas in Parthia and India; Luke in Greece; Simon in Africa and Britain; others in Spain. [1] (Take special note of Simon the Zealot in Britain.)

The first change in the church the way Jesus' own apostles set it up occurred with the leadership. It probably is the greatest problem the church has had from close to the beginning until now. It was usually not the average member who caused worship and organizational problems. Paul had warned that it would be among the leadership that the first apostasy would occur (Acts 20:17, 28-30) and he was right.

It appeared late in the first century. John in Revelation, written about 95 AD, condemned the Nicholaitins. Nicholas means conqueror or ruler, and laity means the common person. The Nicholaitins were developing a clergy-laity system within the church. Jesus was already threatening to take away the lampstand of those congregations (Revelation 1-3).

Every church history written by every denomination recognizes that in the New Testament days, elders, presbyters and bishops were all the same office. They were called by different names in the same way that preacher and evangelist is the same office. In 3rd John 9, this apostle warned about someone who was trying to be the exclusive head of a particular congregation saying that he "loved to have the pre-eminence among them."

INTRODUCED ONE BISHOP BEING OVER
OTHER ELDERS/PRESBYTERS OF A SINGLE
CONGREGATION

NOT WIDELY ACCEPTED

2nd Century

By now, Christianity had also spread further to the region of Mount Ararat in today's Turkey and Russia, and also to France, particularly around Lyons.

About AD 110, Ignatius resurrected the teaching that there was one bishop over the elders of the church, although bishop and elder were the same office in 1st Timothy and Titus, just like congressman and senator is the same office.

Soon after, Ignatius said there should be a bishop over each city, not just his own congregation. In his *Epistle to the Ephesians, 11*, he said the bishop was in charge of the Lord's Supper, or he could allow an elder to do it. This was not accepted in Rome, even in AD 140. It took a hundred years for this system to be universally accepted.

It is interesting that the apostle John wrote 2nd and 3rd John and Revelation around AD 95. Yet in his short letters he identified himself only as "the elder." In Revelation 1:9 he identified himself as merely "brother." Since he was believed to be in Ephesus during his latter years, why did he not call himself the bishop of Ephesus?

INTRODUCED ONE BISHOP PRESIDING OVER ALL
CONGREGATIONS
IN A METROPOLITAN AREA

NOT WIDELY ACCEPTED

About AD 150, the first creed was developed. It was a single sentence which expanded on Jesus' statement that people should be baptized in the name of the Father, the Son, and the Holy Spirit (Matthew 28:19). But about AD 200, it was expanded to include affirmations of Jesus' virgin birth and resurrection from the dead.

The creed was developed because of a second-century group of Christians called Arians who believed that, since Jesus was the created Son of God, he was a lesser God than Jehovah his Father. These people were mostly from northern Africa, especially Egypt and Lybia.

Because differences of opinion began to arise and the apostles were now dead, various people began creating lists of writings (which we today call the New Testament) which were known to be authored by the apostles personally. These individual writings, though actually letters, we today call books.

A generation after the last apostle died, Marcion from northern Turkey compiled a list of 15 apostolic books. Twenty years later another list was compiled that included 23 apostolic books. About 250 AD, Origen in Egypt compiled a list of 21 books which all congregations he had interviewed had accepted, and another list of some they weren't sure about. In 397 AD, a list of 27 books was compiled at a Council in Carthage, North Africa - the same 27 we today call the New Testament.

180 AD is the first mention of baptizing babies. It was not widely accepted by the churches, though a few began to practice it.

INTRODUCED INFANT BAPTISM

NOT WIDELY ACCEPTED

In 187 AD, Victor, the Bishop of Rome, wanted to make that city—the center of the Roman Empire—the central place for celebrating Easter. Irenaeus wrote in the name of the Gallic churches chastising him for his arrogance.

3rd Century

The Bishop of Rome put more pressure on other bishops to fall in line under him because, since Rome was the head of the Roman Empire, Rome should also be head of the church. He continued to meet with a great deal of resistance.

Most often the Bishop of Carthage in North Africa stood as spokesman for the others to maintain independence of each other. Many other bishops of other areas nearby appealed to the Bishop of Carthage to be a spokesman for them in resisting Rome's arrogance.

In 218, Calixtis I, Bishop of Rome, claimed he was Peter's successor. Tertullian, Bishop of Carthage in North Africa and noted Christian writer, called him a usurper in speaking as if he were bishop of bishops.

John Fox who wrote his *Book of Martyrs* said in chapter 2, "It was unfortunate for the Gospel, that many errors had, about this time, crept into the church: the Christians were at variance with each other; self-interest divided those whom social love ought to have united; and the virulence of pride occasioned a variety of factions." [2]

Later he wrote of this same period, "Most of the errors which crept into the church at this time arose from placing human reason in competition with revelation; but the fallacy of such arguments being proved by the most able divines, the opinions they had created vanished away like the stars before the sun" [3]

In 250 when Novatian was voted in as the new Bishop of Rome, many would not accept him, including the powerful Bishop of Carthage, Cyprian. So Novatian tried to get him out of office to put in a new Bishop of Carthage, even though all church offices were considered for life except for voluntary resignations.

Also at this time, substitutes for the form of baptism were introduced, as well as what happened after baptism. The Bishop of Carthage said that people wishing to be baptized where there was insufficient water could, rather than be immersed, have abundant water poured over them three times. Related to that, he also said that a person who was too sick or weak could be baptized by pouring or sprinkling rather than immersion.

INTRODUCED POURING OR SPRINKLING BAPTISM
FOR THE SICK AND WEAK ONLY

NOT WIDELY ACCEPTED

Soon after, people began calling the bishops pontiffs. Today we are told they were called popes which just means papas, but that is not true. Everyone in the Roman Empire knew pontiff is Latin for "bridge-builder" between man and the gods. The title began being used in the Roman Empire 254 BC, some five hundred years earlier. The pontiffs were the senators with all power over both the civil and religious government, and not a body to be mocked by others calling themselves pontiffs.

INTRODUCED BISHOPS BEING CALLED POPES/PONTIFFS

NOT WIDELY ACCEPTED

Further, it was decided the Holy Spirit was not received in baptism, despite the apostle Peter saying it did (Acts 2:38), but rather afterward by the apostles laying on their hands. Since there were no more apostles, they decided the bishops were their successors, it was expected of bishops to lay their hands on people after baptism to deliver the Holy Spirit. This is what they termed "confirmation."

INTRODUCED GIFT OF HOLY SPIRIT CONFERRED
ONLY BY LAYING ON OF HANDS ("CONFIRMATION")
NOT WIDELY ACCEPTED

During this time, a few began saying that the bread and wine of the Lord's Supper was actually the body and blood of Jesus. Because of that, people began bowing to the bread and wine as though bowing to Jesus.

INTRODUCED BREAD & WINE LITERALLY BEING JESUS

NOT WIDELY ACCEPTED

In the meantime in Paris, France, a man named Almericus and six of his disciples were ordered burned at the stake for asserting that Jesus was not present in the sacramental bread of the Lord's Supper, and that it was idolatry to build altars and shrines to saints and to offer incense to them.

The church leadership feud was interrupted in 257 AD when the pagan emperor in Rome, Valerian, made Christian meetings illegal, the first edict of its kind in Rome. After an interlude of peace, under Roman law about 305 AD, copies of Scriptures were ordered destroyed and the few church buildings there were, were confiscated by the government.

4th Century

Around 300, the bishops decided the church universal should be run like the Roman Empire which had an emperor (*pontiff maximus*), then a college of *curia* made up of senators/*pontiffs*, then representatives. A college was any group living under agreed-upon regulations. Therefore, they began what was to be known as the college of cardinals (variation of the Latin word *curia*).

INTRODUCED CHURCH ORGANIZATION
TO FOLLOW
POLITICAL SYSTEM OF ROMAN EMPIRE

NOT WIDELY ACCEPTED

Also they made it official that the bishop would be in charge of priests and deacons in various congregations in surrounding territories around the "mother city."

ORDAINED BISHOP IN CHARGE OF
ALL CONGREGATIONS IN A TERRITORY

The following year, Constantine, whose mother was Christian, was made co-emperor, then emperor of the Roman Empire. Around 304, the gospel was taken to Hungary, then called Pannonia, through Persian Quirinus who had been sent there, and then was martyred.

In 313 a dispute arose between bishops in North Africa over Arianism (the degree of Jesus' divinity), so Constantine called a meeting of the church there in Rome where he had settled. At that time, they declared that Jesus was fully God. Also at that time the term "Roman Catholic" started being used, referring to the universal belief of all Christians in the Roman Empire, not the city of Rome.

A few years later, Constantine moved the capital of the Roman Empire to Istanbul on the border between Italy and today's Turkey, and renamed the city after himself - Constantinople. At that time, he gave the Bishop of Rome, Silvester I, all of southern Italy to rule over as its governor. Thus began the union of church and state. He presented the Lateran Palace that his wife had inherited to the Bishop of Rome. He also gave the Bishop of Rome "all provinces, palaces, and districts of the City of Rome and Italy and of the regions of the West." And he donated a lot of money around the empire for building church buildings.

Now the capital of the Roman Empire was no longer Rome in Italy, but Constantinople in today's Turkey.

The Arians continued preaching that the world was created by an evil god, and only spirit was created by the good God. They also said that, since Jesus was created and in the flesh, he was a lesser God to Jehovah. Other variations of the divine and human nature of Christ continued until about the 8th century. Also confusing was the relationship of God the Father, God the Son, and God the Spirit and the degree of their separateness since God is supposed to be one.

In response to this, in 318 Constantine called a Council meeting in the city of Nicea, Turkey, where the attending bishops formed the Nicean Creed, an expanded version of Matthew 28:19 where Jesus said people were to be baptized in the name of the Father, the Son, and the Holy Spirit. (In 381 they expanded it once more to emphasize the divinity of the Holy Spirit.) People then had to declare their belief in the creed before being baptized.

INTRODUCED THE FIRST OFFICIAL CHURCH CREED

For the rest of the 4th century, it became politically expedient to convert to Christianity because the emperor had. Christians grew then from 10% of the Roman Empire to 90%. Growth was almost too fast to handle. Therefore, bishops of whatever city was the "mother city" (usually the political capital) of each province, became guides to the other bishops of the smaller cities of their province, and so the former began to be called archbishops.

Soon, four "mother cities" were recognized as the most significant Christian centers in the eastern empire, the most honored being Jerusalem. Two others were Alexandria in Egypt and Antioch in Syria, both of which also had connections from the beginning with the apostles. Constantinople, Turkey, the new capital of the Roman Empire, was the fourth "mother city" of the church, but for political reasons.

This escalated the battle between the archbishops/archpopes to see who was most powerful. The two "mother cities" with the most opinionated archbishops were in Rome in Italy and Carthage in northern Africa. But since Carthage had no connection with the apostles, Rome soon won the distinction as "mother city" of the entire western church empire.

GOTHIC TRANSLATION OF THE BIBLE: In 380, Ulifas created the Gothic alphabet. Then he translated the Bible from the Septuagint Greek O.T. and the Greek N.T. Goth is the earliest known Germanic language, and the only east Germanic language. This laid the basis for centuries to come for restoration movements among people who wanted to revert to the simple first-century pattern of the church as opposed to the controlling centralized-government type of church now appearing.

Late in that century, a second Council of Bishops was called to Constantinople. At that time, they declared that the Bishop of Constantinople (the new capital of the Roman Empire) was to be second in importance in the church, second only to the Bishop of

Rome (the original capital of the Roman Empire).

Also in 393, it was limited only to bishops, not to priests or deacons. By then, some were declaring it was more holy not to marry, and pressure began to build for bishops to remain celibate.

INTRODUCED CELIBACY OF BISHOPS

NOT WIDELY ACCEPTED

About this same time there arose more communes of virgins who dedicated themselves to the church. Through the centuries, some men and women had chosen to remain unmarried so they would not be tied down by spouse and children as did the apostle Paul.

As communes of virgin women grew more commonplace, they were recognized and venerated more and more as a special class of Christian. They were considered a Christian version of the pagan Vestal Virgins, priestesses of the goddess Vesta who were highly venerated throughout the Roman Empire even by the senators and emperor himself..

Interestingly, the last temple to Vesta closed in 391 and after 394 there were no more Vestal Virgins. Now the church at Rome got bolder, for it no longer competed with the Roman Empire. The first mention of Christian virgin women living in communes as nuns occurred in a letter of Augustine just before his death in 395 wherein he gave a particular commune instructions on their way of life and organization.

5th Century

In the previous century when unendurable torture and executions of Christians by the pagans ceased, those who had wanted to prove their dedication to God turned to other means of self-destruction. At that time a few in North Africa became self-deprecating hermits with no valuables and no families. This monastery movement gradually spread to others in the Roman Empire, often with several hermits living in the same area but not talking to each other with a vow of silence. This was the beginning of monks.

In 418, some bishops began to baptize infants, declaring they were born in sin.

REINTRODUCED INFANT BAPTISM

STILL NOT WIDELY ACCEPTED

ARMENIAN TRANSLATION OF THE BIBLE: As a result of developing an Armenian (NE Turkish) alphabet, in 422, the New Testament and Proverbs were translated in Armenian. Because they could now read the Bible for themselves, this eventually led to them not agreeing with the Roman church on many things for centuries to come.

In 431 at another Council, the bishops and archbishops officially declared that Mary was originally and still is the Mother of God, and will be forever.

INTRODUCED MARY VENERATION

NOT WIDELY ACCEPTED

During the 5th century, the Roman Empire could no longer defend Britain and northern areas (today's western Europe) from invading Germans, so deserted them. Christians there were left isolated from the rest of the church.

By now the church had spread to Scotland and Ireland, probably as a result of missionary work done by the students of the Apostle Simon in Britain. It is said that Patrick, a Scotsman, established some 250 congregations in Ireland before his death in 493.

In 430, Ninian who had been educated in Rome tried to set up congregations, of course with Roman church beliefs, but met with resistance. Both the Irish and Scottish churches were distinct from the Roman church in many things until they coerced them to live Catholic or face severe persecutions, tortures and deaths.

The practice of book copying (no printing presses yet) was added to the activities of monks in western Europe. This helped with maintaining the Latin translation of the Bible, though it was only available to the clergy.

The Goths, who had never actually been a part of the Roman Empire and who had the Bible translated into their own language, were forced out of their land around the Black Sea by the oriental Huns. Taking their Bible with them, they moved to southern Europe and were the first to sack Rome in 790 years.

As a result of conquering Rome, Augustine in northern Africa wrote his famous *City of God* wherein he tried to build up the wounded egos of Rome's citizens, saying that Rome, as head of the Roman Empire, is the City of Earth. Therefore, Rome, if head of the church, should also be called the City of God.

The displaced Goths moved on into western Europe and finally settled in Gaul, today's France, taking their Bible and first-century Christian views with them. They also invaded and settled in what today is Spain and Switzerland, also taking their Bible with them.

Such spread of the Scriptures in the hands of the people was beginning to alarm the Roman and Constantinople church. Therefore, another Council was called, and in 451 it decreed that no one was allowed to read the Bible for themselves and interpret for themselves. They must accept the interpretation of the church only, or they would be excommunicated.

INTRODUCED BAN ON PRIVATELY INTERPRETING SCRIPTURES

Also, gradually during this century, the clergy began distinguishing their offices from the common Christians by wearing distinctive vestments.

INTRODUCED CLERGY WEARING "HOLY" VESTMENTS

NOT WIDELY ACCEPTED

One other group of Goths moved into modern Netherlands that had closer ties to the Roman church.

6th Century

During the next century, the collapsing Roman Empire was ruled primarily by invading eastern Europeans. Gradually the people of the eastern empire around Constantinople called themselves Byzantine citizens instead of Roman citizens. Each appointed their own bishops who would back their own political power. In 553, the Bishop of Constantinople went against the Bishop of Rome, Justinian, and condemned certain recent actions.

In 573, a rich Italian, Gregory I, was made the mayor of Rome and later Bishop of Rome and called "Gregory the Great." By this time, people all over the Roman Empire had bequeathed farms, vineyards, timber tracts, orchards and so on to the church, but no one had ever done much with them. Subtly he began building his church empire.

With his previous experience as mayor of Rome, Gregory developed all this property to finance the church. When potential invaders approached some of these lands, Gregory took it upon himself to defend the Christians in these areas, thus winning their allegiance. Gradually, he arranged for local church officials who had abused the local people, to fill in for political officials.

Then Gregory began writing the archbishops in Spain, northern Africa, and Greece offering advice and being a friend, and subtly advancing the claim of Rome to supremacy. By this time, Gregory had decided the Bishop of Rome was responsible for all "orthodox" churches, and that all bishops must answer to Rome because this was the seat of the Roman Empire.

When the Bishop of Constantinople announced he was the "Patriarch" of the church, the Bishop of Rome and Gregory both complained it sounded like Constantinople considered itself the most important bishopric in the entire church. However, Rome liked the term Patriarch, and eventually called its leader the Pope/*Pontiff Maximus* of the church. In

This, indeed, was a bold move. The Roman Empire as the world had known it ceased to exist at the end of the 5th century. Before that, the emperors were the *pontiffs maximus*, the high priests, so to speak, of the empire. It had now been close to a hundred years since the fall of the great Roman Empire as the world had known it, and boldness by the Roman church was now in order.

INTRODUCED OFFICE OF POPE/PONTIFF OVER ENTIRE CHURCH

During this time of rising power, Gregory handed over more power to the priests to keep their allegiance by declaring to the people that they must confess their sins in private only to a priest.

He also fed the people with a new symbol of belonging. They were now to make the sign of a cross, either on their forehead or their chest, depending on the occasion.

INTRODUCED CONFESSION TO PRIEST
INTRODUCED MAKING SIGN OF CROSS

NOT WIDELY ACCEPTED

There was also a growing veneration of Mary and martyrs which were also called "saints." Further, they were more and more represented in images. Church leaders assured the people that the images were just to be reminders, not deities, but many people did not make this distinction.

The Bishop of Syria objected to all the bowing down to paintings and statues of Christ, the virgin Mary, apostles and various saints. For the simple people, these representations had become a sort of magic talismen. People bowed before them, burned candles before them, crowned them with flowers, sought miracles from them, and worshipped them.

Late in this century, Boniface of England took the gospel to Germany.

7th Century

In 600 another "Ecumenical Council" was held and it was declared that all edicts of the church carried the same weight as the Four Gospels of the Bible.

ORDAINED CHURCH RULES AS AUTHORITATIVE AS GOSPELS

One of their edicts at this time was to define exactly what was to be said at the mass (Lord's Supper), including reciting the Lord's Prayer.

ORDAINED MASS DIALOGUE

In the meantime, gradually the kings of the various countries in western Europe that Gregory had helped, submitted themselves to the church in Rome except the Christians in the British Isles.

The church in Britain had apparently been founded personally by the apostle Simon (the Zealot) – see endnote once again. They had stayed true to his teachings all this time. So when the Roman church arrived, they refused to submit to celibacy of the clergy, confession to priests, and purgatory.

At the beginning of the 7th Century, Gregory sent missionaries to the British Isles to represent him. The Christians in the British Isles did not take kindly to Gregory's presumptuousness. However, gradually the Christians in England agreed to follow the direction of the church in Rome.

Back in earlier centuries, the Franks (former Germans) in the Netherlands, helped Rome fight off the Huns from the Orient, and later the Muslims from the Middle East. So, although the kings declared allegiance to Rome, they were so lazy that the Franks were able to move in and run the countries for them. So, by the middle of the 7th century, there was once again a division as to whether to submit to the Roman church or not.

In the late 7th century, the Franks began sending out missionaries to convert the pagans in western Europe. Boniface of England was their most influential missionary. He traveled into Germany and parts of central Europe, and finally France. He was so effective that Rome claimed him as an ally and representative also. The Franks claimed much of the land previously donated to the church to be now under their control.

Also during this time down in Italy, the Lombards were trying to unite and take over the now-splintered country. Pope Gregory III was unwilling to cooperate, so asked the Byzantines in Constantinople to help. They wouldn't because they did not want to give up the power they already had in Italy. He also asked the Franks for help, and they, too, declined.

The next generation of Franks decided they did not want to be rulers just in act, but also in name. They appealed to the patriarch of Rome, the pope, for endorsement and got it. The first Frankish king—Pepin— was crowned and anointed in a religious ceremony.

At that same time the Lombards took over land in Italy, claiming Rome also. Pope Stephen went to France for help which he obtained from Pepin. They became allies when the pope personally recrowned King Pepin.

When that king died, his son succeeded him—Charles the Great, also known as Charlemagne. He helped the pope regain control of Italy and gave back much of the church land to Rome. When the Lombards tried one last time to take over Rome, King Charles/Charlemagne came down and got rid of the Lombards and made himself king of Italy, but left control of Rome to the pope.

Charlemagne also sent missionaries into the British Isles (Saxony) which they resisted. For resisting him, he finally had 4,500 Saxon warriors beheaded in one day.

In 666, Pope St. Vitalian introduced the use of the organ in worship in Rome to improve on singing. A second organ was placed in France in 757, and a third one also in France in 812. About that same time, a fourth one was placed in Germany. So one organ was introduced per century.

INTRODUCED INSTRUMENTAL MUSIC

NOT WIDELY ACCEPTED

In 692, the church in Rome officially declared that priests who were promoted to bishop had to leave their wives to become celibate, but their wives could become deaconesses and live elsewhere.

ORDAINED FORMER WIVES OF BISHOPS
MADE DEACONESSES

8th Century

OLD ENGLISH TRANSLATION OF THE BIBLE: In Great Britain, Caedmon, referring to the Latin translation of the Bible, paraphrased the Bible in poetry form in the common language of the people. Also near this time, Bede made an actual translation of the Bible based on the Latin translation.

In the year 700, the western church in Rome declared that Mary was the mediator between man and her Son, Jesus. This view was adopted thirty years later by the eastern church in Constantinople.

ORDAINED MARY IS THE MEDIATOR BETWEEN
MAN AND JESUS

Also in this century, it was decreed that only the Bishop of Rome was to be called Pope. This, of course, made the powerful Bishop of Constantinople in Turkey angry. The rift between them grew.

ORDAINED PAPACY EXCLUSIVELY IN ROME

Worship Changes Since the First Century

In the meantime, Leo III became Emperor of the Roman Empire in Constantinople in 717. He successfully drove the Muslims back out of Europe, though they had succeeded in taking the Middle East.

However, the Muslims continually accused the Christians of idol worship, referring to paintings and carvings of Christ and the "saints." In 726 Leo III called a Council of bishops and senators demanding their complete removal from church buildings, and that church murals be covered with plaster.

Horrified worshippers attacked soldiers trying to enforce the edict. The Patriarch of Constantinople did not want the pictures and carvings removed either, so Emperor Leo deposed him. At the same time, Pope Gregory II in Rome anathematized (cursed) Leo. Those who refused the use of pictures and carvings were accused of denying the incarnation of Jesus as a human.

In 757, Rome having lost control of Italy in earlier centuries, King Pepin and his son, Charlemagne, gave control of Italy back to the pope.

In 767 the next Patriarch of Constantinople was beheaded for favoring the pictures and carvings. Monasteries were confiscated by the government and resisting monks were imprisoned and tortured, eyes or tongues torn out, and noses cut off. At Ephesus the governor ordered monks and nuns to marry each other or be killed.

But in 787 the edict was reversed at Nicea and the veneration—though not the worship—of pictures and carvings was restored. They officially approved bowing down to statues of saints, holy men, the cross, Jesus, Mary, and angels.

ORDAINED BOWING TO IMAGES

Still, the rift between the eastern church in Constantinople and the western church in Rome grew.

Some time later, a new pope was elected in Rome—Leo III. But he was so corrupt that he was beaten on a deserted road and imprisoned in a monastery. His friends helped him escape and he went to Britain to get Charlemagne to side with him. Charlemagne went with him back to Rome for a trial where the evidence against him was overwhelming. But Charlemagne said if Leo swore he was innocent, then he would be.

A few days later, while Charlemagne was kneeling in prayer at the front of the church building, Pope Leo surprised him by taking a crown that was on the altar, placing it on Charlemagne's head, and announcing he had been crowned by God. This was the official beginning of the "Holy Roman Empire" although not called by this name until 300 years later.

Charlemagne was surprised and a little upset by this, but did not turn it down. But when he gave up his kingship to his son, Louis, he crowned his son himself. This brought up the question as to whether the pope makes the emperor or the emperor makes the pope.

Yet Charlemagne always remained supportive of the Roman church. He used political authority to suppress heresy, to collect tithes of the people, guarantee discipline of the clergy, developed a distinctive dress for the clergy, and made sure all churches followed the Roman "liturgy" in all their services. He also developed cathedral schools to train the clergy, imported scholars to teach in monasteries, and had cantors trained to sing Gregorian chants in the church.

After his death, his son, Louis was recrowned by the visiting pope. This gesture was made to infer it was the church in Rome who had made him king. After this, the pope showed up at other coronations of other kings in Europe and crowned them too. Thus grew the idea that the crown had been conferred by the papacy.

King Louis divided his empire among his three sons to rule. But when a fourth son was born and he tried to redivide the kingdom, his three sons rose up against him. Pope Gregory IV sided with the sons, and King Louis ended up powerless. By the end of the 9th century, Charlemagne's empire had been divided into Germany, France, and the Netherlands running south into Italy.

The Frankish bishops felt the pope had no right to interfere with politics. The pope quoted Matthew 16:19 where Jesus gave the keys of the kingdom to Peter, and the bishops retorted with Matthew 18:18 where he gave the keys to all the apostles. Thus began a dispute and popular resistance that would build up eventually to the Reformation 600 years later.

Besides fighting between politicians and between churchmen, there was fighting between politicians and churchmen. So in Le Mans, France, in 857, some clerics got together and produced a series of documents—some of which were fabricated and forged—that they claimed came out of Seville 200 years earlier and proved the papacy approved.

These *Pseudo-Isidorian Decretals* were made up of documents, letters and decrees of bishops and Councils of the 2nd and 3rd centuries exalting the power of the pope. These forged papers were used to prove papal supremacy over all bishops with no interference by the laity or politicians. By the time these papers were recognized as forgeries centuries later, they had already done their damage.

9th Century

During this century, Radbertus and other church leaders began writing and teaching at length that the bread and wine of the Lord's Supper became the literal body and blood of Jesus. But they still met with a great deal of resistance.

GERMAN TRANSLATION OF THE BIBLE: This translation was made from the Vulgate, translator unknown.

SLAVONIC TRANSLATION OF THE BIBLE: Cyril and Methodius, missionaries from Constantinople to Moravia, invented a Slavic alphabet which was later called the Cyrillic alphabet. They translated the Bible from the Greek *Septuagint* O.T. and the Greek N.T. into the language of the people. It was called the *Old church Slavonic Bible*.

In 850, it was decided people should sprinkle themselves or be sprinkled by a priest every Sunday as they entered their place of worship. The water must be blessed by the priest, which then turned it into holy water.

ORDAINED WEEKLY HOLY WATER

Also about this time, the church bishops decided that people receiving the Lord's Supper had to make a sign of the cross before partaking. They also decided the bread of the Lord's Supper had to be placed directly on the tongues of the congregation, and only by a bishop.

ORDAINED SIGN OF CROSS AT LORD'S SUPPER
ORDAINED BISHOP MUST PLACE BREAD ON CONGREGATION'S TONGUES

Further, by this time, the number of holy vestments worn by the clergy had increased to seven specific parts of garments. More and more these vestments gained ornateness during the following centuries.

ORDAINED CLERGY WEAR HOLY VESTMENTS

King Boris of Bulgaria was converted to Christianity in 865. He did not know whether to side with the Patriarch of Constantinople or the Pope of Rome. The Patriarch said services could be held in the Slavonic language, so King Boris sided with Constantinople. This widened the rift between Constantinople and Rome.

In 869, the Pope of Rome excommunicated the Patriarch of Constantinople, who in turn excommunicated the former. This was the last time the churches of the east represented in Constantinople ever met in official Council with the churches of the west represented in Rome. Up until now, all such Councils had been held in or near Constantinople and in the Greek language.

During this century in Rome, strong popes and weak popes emerged. Pope John VIII was poisoned and then bludgeoned to death in his bed in 882. Pope Marinus I was assassinated. Next came Pope Stephen VII.

In 897 with the blessing of Pope Stephen, the body of an

earlier pope, Formosus, was exhumed, clothed in papal robes and put on trial for heresy. His three fingers used to bestow the papal blessing were cut off, his papal robes stripped off, and his corpse dragged through Rome and cast into the Tiber River. Later that year Pope Stephen was strangled.

10th Century

The next pope lasted only four months, and the next only 20 days. Pope Leo V was elected in 903 but killed two months later. His assassin then made himself pope - something that official Roman Catholic lists do not recognize.

The assassin was killed by Sergius III who then became pope. Sergius took a 13-year-old mistress, Marozia, daughter of the political leader of Rome. She bore Pope Sergius a son. After his death, the matron of the political family, Theodora, appointed the next three popes. The eyes of John X were put out by the next political head of Rome; he was imprisoned and died there a year later.

In 927 the pope's widow Marozia took over the city of Rome and appointed the next three popes, the third one being John XI, the illegitimate son of herself and Pope Sergius. Marozia's first legitimate son conquered his mother and threw Pope John XI into prison. Just prior to his death, he forced the Roman Senate to make his son Octavian the next pope; and he ruled under the name John XII.

Pope John XII had many mistresses and freely used church contributions to finance personal enjoyments. He was even known to have raped some of the female pilgrims at St. Peter's. He was so immoral that at this point, the church decided that the infallibility of the pope did not involve his personal life, but only his official church pronouncements.

In 973, the Roman church canonized the first "saint," a practice that continues even today. Before that, as far back as the 3rd century, pictures and statues were made of people who had been martyred and called saints as a title. Controversy over bowing down to their pictures and statues clouded the issue. But now it was declared that a saint had to be dead and to have performed a provable miracle.

ORDAINED CANONIZATION OF THE FIRST SAINT

In 977, the Bohemians requested that Pope Benedict VII allow them to have services in their own language, and that the cup of the Lord's Supper to given to the laity also. The pope granted both. But succeeding popes reneged on both.

OLD ENGLISH TRANSLATION OF THE BIBLE: In 995, Aelfric wrote so many homilies on the Old and New Testaments that he ended up quoting most of it, and did translate all of the Hexateuch from Latin.

Meanwhile, the title of Holy Roman Emperor moved from western Europe around France to eastern Europe around Germany. Otto I had too many in his family wanting his crown, so he turned to bishops and archbishops to help govern his kingdom. To solidify the power he gave them, Otto gave large parcels of land to each. As a result, he also insisted on playing a major role in selecting the bishops.

This led to his interest in who was pope. In 964, an irate husband beat Pope John XII so badly when he discovered him in bed with his wife, that the pope died three days later. After this, Emperor Otto supervised appointments to the papacy. Even Otto's grandson, Otto III, appointed his cousin Bruno who changed his name to Pope Gregory V. This was the first German pope. When Gregory V was poisoned in 999, Otto installed his former French tutor Sylvester II as pope.

In 1002 Otto was poisoned and the following year Pope Sylvester II was poisoned. The next emperor, Henry II, was not interested in the papacy.

Late in this century, the Grand Duke of what we today call Russia was converted to Christianity. He married the sister of the Byzantine Emperor, then introduced the Eastern church to his country where it remains strong to this day. Another rift with Rome.

11th Century

In 1000 in France, a man named Berengarius preached Gospel truths according to the primitive ways of the first century. Later Peter Bruis taught similarly, with followers separating from the church of Rome. He wrote a book against the pope entitled ANTICHRIST.

In 1010, Peter de Bruys and his followers called Petrobusians in France, rejected the mass, held that the Lord's Supper was a memorial, and that ministers should marry. Simultaneously, a monk Henry was baptized and began preaching the same thing. His followers were called by outsiders Henricians. They considered themselves the church of Christ

During these years of power plays by the various popes, many new decrees were put on the Christians by the bishops. As of 1014, priests had to chant the Nicean Creed (decree) at the Lord's Supper.

ORDAINED CHANTING OF NICEAN CREED REQUIRED AT LORD'S SUPPER (MASS)

In 1018, the church decided to force all priests and deacons to be celibate. If they insisted on being married, their children of the marriage were made lifetime slaves of the church, never to be freed.

ORDAINED PRIESTS & DEACONS NOT MARRY
ORDAINED CHILDREN OF PRIESTS TO BE SLAVES OF CHURCH

The next three popes were appointed by the Italian Crescenti family, and the following three by the Tusculum family. The latter three were brothers and a nephew. Benedict VIII bought his office with open bribery. Pope John XIX bought the papacy and, being a layman, passed through all the clerical degrees in one day. Benedict IX was 12 years old and eventually committed murders and adulteries in broad daylight, and robbed pilgrims to Rome.

After three others were declared pope simultaneously with him, Benedict IX voluntarily resigned in 1045, but sold the papacy to his Jewish god-father who became Gregory VI. When the previous two popes wanted their papacy back, Emperor Henry III returned and deposed them all, appointing another German pope.

In 1049, with some priests still marrying, the church decided that all their wives and concubines were to be made servants of the church.

ORDAINED PRIEST'S WIVES TO BE SERVANTS OF CHURCH

In the mid 11th century, when southern Italy was invaded by Viking Normans, Pope Leo IX personally led troops to push them back out. The Viking Normans won and imprisoned Pope Leo IX for nine months; he died a month later in Rome. But by now King Philip of France, King William II of England, and King Henry IV of Germany were all excommunicated.

Meanwhile, in 1053 in Constantinople, the patriarch closed down all Latin monasteries and churches. In the process of closing down one of the churches, the soldiers walked on the bread used in the Lord's Supper. According to Roman beliefs, they had walked on the actual body of Christ.

Then the patriarch issued an open letter to the pope, although addressed to the bishops and priests of France, objecting to Roman beliefs such as fasting on Saturday, eating meat strangled with the blood still in it, and barring priests from marrying.

Thereupon Roman papal delegates put a written anathema (curse) on the patriarch and all his followers. These events are today called the Great Schism. Basically, the split between eastern and western church headquarters was complete and final and exists even today: The Western Roman Catholic church and the Eastern Orthodox church. Only periodically when it benefited both sides, did the two unite.

Remember, the pope at this time was the *pontiff maximus*, carrying the same title as the Caesars who were the high priests of the official Roman religion as well as emperors over the citizens and slaves of the realm. Up until now, all popes had been appointed by whoever was the strongest king or family either in Rome or all of Europe.

Within the Roman Empire, the college of pontiffs (senators) elected the next Caesar, although some Caesars declared the title by reason of political strength.

In 1059, it was decided that the Pope/Pontiff of Rome must be elected by the cardinals, this group being a copy of the Roman senate who used to elect the emperor.

ORDAINED CARDINALS ELECT POPE/PONTIFF MAXIMUS

In 1075 a decree was renewed condemning priest marriages, fornication, and purchasing church office. This was an indirect blow to monarchs appointing their own bishops.

King Henry IV refused to conform, so the church began excommunicating his bishops. Therefore, Pope Gregory excommunicated King Henry IV and told him he was no longer king. Thereupon, King Henry marched to Rome and captured the pope. He was rescued two years later but died in exile a year after that.

In 1066, the Viking Normans invaded England. At first the English ruler appointed his own bishops as the others had, but a compromise was finally reached wherein the pope's representative crowned the king and the king's representative granted the bishop with land. This trend then moved east across Europe to Germany.

WEST SAXON TRANSLATION OF THE BIBLE: Around this same time, the Four Gospels were translated from Latin into the language of West Saxony which today is the western part of Germany and the Netherlands.

In 1079, the church officially declared that the bread and wine of the Lord's Supper are substantially changed into the body and blood of Jesus (trans-substantiation), and therefore worshippers had to bow down to these emblems as though bowing before Jesus in person.

ORDAINED BREAD & WINE ACTUALLY

BECOMES JESUS
ORDAINED BOWING TO BREAD & WINE

Also about this time, it was decided to have both candles and incense in the mass (Lord's Supper).

INTRODUCED CANDLES IN WORSHIP

NOT WIDELY ACCEPTED

INTRODUCED INCENSE IN WORSHIP

NOT WIDELY ACCEPTED

By 1095, the Muslims had conquered the entire Middle East and killed Christian pilgrims who dared go to their Holy Land. They also took much of Turkey where Constantinople was. (The Apostle Paul, by the way, established most of the first-century congregations in Turkey.) The patriarch sent for help from the pope.

Pope Urban II promised that all who would volunteer for a crusade against the Muslims that they would receive remission of the guilt of all sins and be tax-exempt. He even allowed prisoners to be released so they could join.

This was the beginning of indulgences. Later indulgences were allowed for just equipping someone to go on a crusade. An indulgence is not forgiveness of sins, but a way of paying the penalty for sins by paying money, serving in the church military, or anything assigned by the pope, rather than having to pay for it in purgatory or hell.

ORDAINED PAYMENT OF INDULGENCES

In this first Crusade, peasant troops, loosely organized by

two monks, did not wait for the professional military, but headed across Europe toward the Holy Land. Without proper preparation, they ended up pillaging village after village for food and money, and often raped the women while they were at it. When they arrived in eastern Turkey to take it back from the Muslims, they were annihilated.

A more organized group of 30,000 dukes, mostly from France, took their troops as far as Tarsus in Turkey. There someone claimed to have discovered the spear that had pierced Jesus' side. This inspired the troops so much that they conquered the Muslims in that area.

During this century, the church at Rome declared that the laity should not drink the wine of the Lord's Supper. They could only have the bread.

ORDAINED LAITY CANNOT DRINK WINE OF LORD'S SUPPER (MASS)

12th Century

In 1118 the Knights Templar was founded in Jerusalem, a military order associated with the pope to protect pilgrims from the Muslims. After the crusades, they returned to Europe, mostly France.

After 150 years in France, those wanting primitive Christianity as described only in the Bible began to be led by Henry of Toulouse. In 1147 he announced they would not admit any proofs regarding religion unless they were from the Scriptures themselves. These Henericians were named heretics by the pope. They just wanted to be known as the church of Christ.

Not long after, Peter Waldo of Lyons picked up this movement, and the followers were then called Waldenses, a name that some still carry in the 21st century.

During this time, Bernard of Clairvaux wrote what would later be set to music to feed the spiritual hunger of Christians centuries later. Among them were:

> Jesus, the very thought of Thee
> With sweetness fills my breast;
> But sweeter far Thy face to see,
> And in Thy presence rest.
>
> and
>
> Jesus, Thou joy of loving hearts,
> Thou Fount of life, Thou Light of men,
> From the best bliss that earth imparts,
> We turn unfilled to Thee again.
>
> Thy truth unchanged hath ever stood;
> Thou savest those that on Thee call;
> To them that seek Thee, Thou art good,
> To them that find Thee, all in all!

With Pope Adrian, in 1154 persecution arose in Italy. A German named Arnold visited Rome and preached against the corruptions and additions that had been made to the New Testament church by the church at Rome. The pope ordered him to leave Rome, so he returned to Germany and kept preaching the same thing.

One of three royalty of Germany owed the pope a favor and returned Arnold to him. There at Apulia, he and his friends were burned at the stake.

Encenas, a Spaniard raised in Rome, began preaching against the papacy. He was arrested for having a New Testament in Spanish and imprisoned. He escaped and fled to Germany.

Faninus became a protestant Waldense and preached to others. He was arrested and sentenced to death. His executioners were amazed at his remarkable happiness. He replied that Jesus' suffering and death freed his followers from fear of the same. He was then strangled and burned.

Dominicus, a soldier, became a protestant and preached the Gospel in its purity. When arrested and asked, "Will you renounce your doctrines?" he replied, "My doctrines! I maintain no doctrines of my own; what I preach are the doctrines of Christ, and for those I will forfeit my blood, and even think myself happy to suffer for the sake of my Redeemer." He was then tortured and hanged.

Galeacius near St. Angelo, preached against the papacy. **He was arrested and burned to death.**

In the middle of this century, Bernard of Cluny (Chany) and Morlaix, an English-Frenchman, wrote this hymn:

> *Jerusalem the golden, with milk and honey blest,*
> *Beneath thy contemplation sink heart and voice opprest....*
> *They stand, those halls of Zion, all jubilant with song,*
> *So bright with many an angel and all the martyr throng.*

At the same time, the Roman church ordered that laity not be permitted to read Scriptures. Both efforts failed to eliminate them. Instead, their numbers grew, not only in France, but throughout Europe.

The pope sent for volunteers all over Europe to get rid of the Albigenses, and promised paradise to anyone who joined his Holy War for forty days.

DURING THIS CENTURY, BAPTISM BY POURING
BEGAN TO BE WIDELY ACCEPTED

In 1177, the church determined the minimum age for a bishop be thirty. It also decided that the pope must have a two-thirds approval of the cardinals to be elected.

ORDAINED MINIMUM AGE FOR BISHOPS
ORDAINED ELECTION PERCENTAGE FOR POPES

In 1198 Innocent III became pope and was the most politically powerful pope in history. He was the first to declare that he was the representative of Christ both in the church and in the entire world. Before this, at the beginning the 6th century, various bishops calls themselves Vicars of Christ. Now it was narrowed down to one human in Rome.

ORDAINED POPE IS VICARIOUSLY
CHRIST ON EARTH

To regain control of "the earth," he manipulated future kings of Germany and France, but he could not control King John of England. So he excommunicated the King of England and refused to allow any Englishman to celebrate any of the sacraments.

About this time, Bernard of Clairvaux, France, wrote this which was set to music four centuries later and is sung throughout the world today:

> *O sacred head, now wounded*
> *With grief and shame weighed down;*
> *How art Thou pale with anguish,*
> *With sore abuse and scorn;*
>
> *How does that visage languish*
> *Which once was bright as morn!*
> *What language shall I borrow*
> *To thank Thee, dearest Friend,*
>
> *For this Thy dying sorrow,*
> *Thy pity without end?*
> *O make me Thine forever;*
> *And should I fainting be,*
>
> *Lord, let me never, never*
> *Outlive my love to Thee.*

One of Pope Innocent's earlier teachers, Huguccio of Bologna, came to believe that the pope could err, so the church should actually be run by a Council representing all the members, and the pope had to obey the Council. This was the seed of a Reformation Movement called "conciliarism" referring to Councils ruling the church. But few people had the courage to agree with him.

Innocent offered indulgences to troops who marched on his behalf to protect southern Italy and to conquer "heretics" in southern France. This would be his second crusade.

Also that year the pope solicited help for a third crusade which was organized among knights of various countries. In 1212 was the Children's Crusade. King Andrew of Hungry launched another crusade in 1217 after the Fourth Lateran Council declared it. The sixth crusade was led by Emperor Frederick II of Spain in 1227.

The seventh crusade was led by King Louis IV of France in 1249. The eighth crusade was led by Prince Edward of England. This last crusade was the final one. Then the European Christians left the Holy Land in the control of the Muslims.

It was during this time that a "Christmas" hymn was written (no one celebrated Christmas at this time.)

> O come, O come, Emmanuel,
> And ransom captive Israel....
> O come, Thou Branch of Jesse's stem,
> Unto Thine own, and rescue them!

ENDNOTES

[1]. Cruse, Christian F., Translator, *The Ecclesiastical History of Eusebius Pamphilus*, Baker Book House, 1955, pg. 42-43, 48-51, 58, 63-65, 82, 101-107, 116-117; AND Forbush, William B., editor, *Fox's Book of Martyrs*, Zondervan Publishing House, 1968, pg. 1-5

[2]. Fox, pg. 14

[3]. Fox, pg. 18

BIBLIOGRAPHY

D'Aubigne, J. H. Merle, *History of the Reformation of the Sixteenth Century*, The Religious Tract Society, London, 1846

The Ecclesiastical History of Eusebius Pamphilus, Baker Book House, Grand Rapids, 1971

Encyclopedia Britannica, William Benton Publisher, Chicago, 1966

Forbush, William B., Editor, *Fox's Book of Martyrs*, Zondervan Publishing House, Grand Rapids, 1926

Goold, G. P., Editor, *Bede Historical Works: Ecclesiastical History of the English Nation*, Vol. I and II

Keyes, Nelson B., *Story of the Bible World*, Reader's Digest Assn, Pleasantville, NY, 1962

Lightfoot, J.B., Editor, *The Apostolic Fathers*, Baker Book House, Grand Rapids, 1965

McDonald, William J., Editor, *The New Catholic Encyclopedia*, McGraw-Hill, Chicago, 1962

North, James B., *From Pentecost to the Present*, College Press Publishing, Joplin, Mo., 1983

Simon, Edith, *Great Ages of Man: The Reformation*, Time-Life Books, NY, 1968

Burrage, Henry S., [Ana]*Baptist Hymn Writers and their Hymns*, Brown Thurston & Co., Portland, Maine, 1889

Wells, H.G., *The Outline of History*, Garden City Books, NY, 1961

2. CHANGES IN WORSHIP

13th to 16th Centuries

13th Century

To get his kingdom back, King John of England, gave in to the pope in 1213, gave him all the land in England, and became England's puppet ruler.

About this time, Pope Innocent III declared that incense be used in exorcisms.

INTRODUCED INCENSE IN EXORCISMS

In 1215, the church officially decreed that the bread and wine of the Lord's Supper became the actual body and blood of Jesus. They also declared everyone should receive communion at least once a year. Also they approved having a crucifix (cross with Jesus on it) on the table with the Lord's Supper.

ORDAINED BREAD & WINE ACTUALLY JESUS
ORDAINED LORD'S SUPPER TO BE TAKEN
AT LEAST YEARLY

INTRODUCED CRUCIFIX ON COMMUNION
TABLE (ALTAR)

NOT WIDELY ACCEPTED

A group of people in southern France, the Albenses, denied Jesus' virgin birth, were celibates, and did not take the New Testament literally.

Therefore, Pope Innocent, between 1209 and 1218 massacred men, women, children and elderly until he had annihilated them. Indulgences were allowed for anyone joining the pope's troops to carry out the slaughter.

In 1230 during the time of Pope Gregory IX, canonization of certain Christians by declaring them "saints" was officially adopted by the Roman church.

During the Roman Empire, heroic humans were declared gods by vote of the pontiffs (senate) and approval by the *pontiff maximus* (emperor). Tradition says Pilate submitted the name of Jesus to the Roman senators/pontiffs to be officially declared a god. The same pattern of voting and final approval of the pope/*pontiff maximus* is still being followed to declare a dead Christian a saint, this despite the Bible calling all Christians saints.

ORDAINED CANONIZATION OF SAINTS

In 1245 the idea of purgatory was introduced as a way to get people to pay indulgences to get their loved ones out of purgatory and into heaven.

INTRODUCED PURGATORY

NOT WIDELY ACCEPTED

In 1274, the church insisted that believers must not only be baptized, but they must be confirmed with laying on of a bishop's hands to receive the Holy Spirit ("confirmation").

ORDAINED HOLY SPIRIT BE IMPARTED AFTER BAPTISM

At this time, also, the church decided to Anglicize and transliterate the Greek word, "Presbyter" in the Bible and call them presbyters/elders, priests.

ORDAINED THAT PRESBYTERS ARE PRIESTS

ITALIAN TRANSLATION OF THE BIBLE: During this century, the Waldenses escaped to Italy. There they translated the Bible into the language of the Italian people.

DUTCH/NETHERLANDS TRANSLATION OF THE BIBLE: During this century, several translations of the Bible into the common language of the people in the Netherlands came into being, names of translators unknown.

Late in this century, King Edward I of England, called the Model Parliament where representatives of the people ruled and recommended to the monarch what he should do.

About that same time, Dominican John of Paris announced that the authority of the church did not rest on its head alone but on every member through representatives. But people were afraid to agree with him in public and take the chance of losing their souls. Things were not bad enough yet.

In 1299, Pope Innocent III declared that it was a sin to study the Bible alone without interpretation by the Roman church.

ORDAINED IT A SIN TO STUDY BIBLE
WITHOUT CLERGY

14th Century

In 1303, King Philip IV of France assembled the first Estates General, representatives of the church, royalty, and commoners. This was more food for thought on how to rule the church at a time when the pope was taking advantage of the members.

Pope Boniface VIII tried unsuccessfully to make the clergy tax-exempt in England and France. After several other run-ins, King Philip IV of France had Pope Boniface captured by his men in 1303. The pope died a month later.

The next pope, Benedict XI was poisoned after nine months in office. The next pope was a Frenchman and friend of King Philip, and consented to being crowned pope in France to heal relationships between the two rulers.

Because the political climate in Rome was anti-papal, Benedict settled on the Rhone River in Avignon, France, and the papacy stayed there for 70 years. The next six popes were also French. During this time there was a great deal of graft on the papal staff, even to paying to see the pope, and putting the pope's relatives in church office. The papacy grew more and more wealthy.

Further, to finance personal luxuries, Pope John XXII demanded a tithe of all clerical income, received the first year's income from new officials, claimed for himself the house and goods of deceased bishops, demanded love offerings from the people, rented out papal land, claimed the income of any church office that was vacant, and a tax of one penny per household in more than a dozen European countries.

MIDDLE ENGLISH TRANSLATIONS OF THE BIBLE: In the middle of this century, John Purvey and Nicholas of Hereford translated the Bible into the language of the common person in England. However, they did not get much circulation.

During this time, Marsilius of Padua and William of Ockham publicly resurrected the idea of Conciliarism - the church being run by Councils who represented the people. They claimed the bishop and papal system was not founded by Christ but developed through time. But this was not a good time to speak against the pope.

In 1343, the church made an official decree that indulgences must be paid for punishment of sins.

ORDAINED INDULGENCES FOR SINS

In 1367, Pope Urban V ordered the papal palace in Rome repaired, then returned to Rome. In 1378 Italian Pope Urban VI was elected under threat of insurrection by the Italians. Then the French cardinals declared his papacy invalid and elected Clement VII, a Frenchman, a pope. Europe now chose sides; excommunications and massacres were perpetuated for both. From now on for many years, the people would be divided between the pope in Rome and the pope In Avignon, France.

What made it more glaring is that they were about evenly

divided—two popes in the north (Europe), and a third in the south—Turkey.

The chaos in church leadership and insistence on paying indulgences were the "straw that broke the camel's back" for many. For years people had been thinking there had to be a better way. Now they felt forced to not only think about it, but perhaps try to do something about it. But they needed a leader. Who could he be?

GERMAN TRANSLATION OF THE BIBLE: In 1366, the Bible was translated literally word for word from the Latin into the common language of the people in Germany. It was this Bible that, a century later, would be the first one reproduced on a printing press.

By this time, the idea that the pope and cardinals should answer to a general Council of representatives was being taught also by Henry of Langenstein and Konrad of Gelnhausen in Germany.

When the laity in Bohemia tried to form such a Council, Pope Gregory XI heard about it and banished everyone involved, then put additional religious restraints on the people.

At this time John Wyclif, wrote, "They blaspheme who extol the pope above all that is called God." He trained preachers who traveled all over England preaching in the people's language, reading directly from the Gospels and Epistles, and teaching the Ten Commandments and other basic tenets of the Bible.

Soon after, Wyclif rose up to represent those wanting to return to only the rules in the New Testament of the Bible with its headquarters in heaven. He denied that the bread and wine became the actual body and blood of Jesus, and he declared the pope was the Antichrist. He also declared that only elders and deacons were to be officers in the church that Jesus established. He also said that the elders were the same as presbyters, priests, and bishops. By 1380 he was saying that all Christians were priests.

"He condemned the cult of the saints, relics, and pilgrimages. He repudiated indulgences and masses for the dead, although he retained belief in purgatory." [1]

MIDDLE ENGLISH TRANSLATION OF THE BIBLE: In 1380 John Wyclif translated the Bible into English from the Latin version, almost word for word. His was successful.

His followers, the "Lollards", though they called themselves the church of Christ, used his New Testament to preach everywhere they went. In 1382 papal decrees were enacted against him, and the Council of Constance formally condemned 267 of his tenets. (Years after he died, representatives of the pope exhumed his bones, burned them, and threw his ashes into a river.)

Wyclif was later called "The Morning Star of the Reformation." He died in 1384.

Sometime during this century, one of our Christian brothers wrote this hymn that would be set to music three centuries later:

> *Jesus Christ is risen today, Al-le-lu-ia!*
> *Our triumphant holy day, Al-le-lu-ia!*
> *Who did once upon the cross, Al-le-lu-ia!*
> *Suffer to redeem our loss, Al-le-lu-ia!*

In the meantime, in 1393, the University of Paris formally sent a letter to King Charles VI of France saying they would form a general Council to get control of the church if both popes did not resign immediately. Of course, neither pope gave up their power. Just before the end of the century, theologians at the University of Paris called for King Charles to withdraw his support of the pope in Avignon, France.

ANGLO-NORMAN TRANSLATION OF THE BIBLE: This translation was done in part, but never completed. The Anglo-Normans were of Viking descent and lived mostly in the northern part of France.

15th Century

This could be called the bloody century, except it will not stop here. The blood of Christians just trying to follow the New Testament will continue until the movement finally escapes to America some 300 years later.

Two years after Wyclif's death, King Richard of England married the sister of the King of Bohemia. With such ties, many from Bohemia studied at Oxford in England, then returned to the

University of Prague, taking Wyclif's ideas of reform with them.

When John Huss entered the University of Prague, he saw Wyclif's writings and rewrote them for his own use. He was ordained a priest in 1400.

Appointed preacher of a Prague chapel, Huss's sermons were both in Latin and Czech. He condemned church corruptions, said Christ and not Peter was the foundation of the church, and also taught moral reform to his people.

In 1401, the King of England ordered that all of Wyclif's followers, called Lollards, be burned as heretics. William Santree of Smithfield was the first to be burned. In 1419, Sir John Oldcastle, was sentenced burned. In 1473, Thomas Granter was burned at the stake outside London. In 1499, Badram was burned in Norwich.

ROMANIAN TRANSLATION OF THE BIBLE: In 1405, Nicodim translated the four gospels into the language of the common people. They were located east of the Black Sea near Russia.

In 1410, Pope Alexander V in Avignon, France, prohibited preaching in private chapels and for Wyclif's books to be burned. But Huss continued to preach, supported by his king, queen, university, and the citizens of Prague in Czechoslovakia.

In the meantime, in Italy, a Council was called to meet at Pisa to solve the problem of two of the three popes - the two being in Europe. Protected by King Charles VI of France, 1000 churchmen and other interested people including ambassadors from England, Poland, France, Portugal, Bohemia, Sicily and smaller areas assembled.

This Council summoned both popes, but they refused to come. So the Council deposed them and elected a fourth pope - Alexander V! But Pope Alexander V died less than a year later. So the Council elected another pope - John XXIII. He, with his army, took over Rome, driving out Pope Gregory, but only temporarily.

When John XXIII took over as pope in Avignon, France, in 1410, he began selling indulgences to raise money for a crusade against Naples. Huss attacked the pope. Two years later Pope John excommunicated Huss.

Pope John XXIII was so bad, that some 200 maidens, nuns and married women fell victims to his passions. He violated virgins, lived in adultery, was guilty of sodomy, sold cardinal offices to children of wealthy families, and denied both heaven and hell.

Angered, the Council met again, but this time in Constance, Switzerland. About 20,000 attended. There they had the support of even more world leaders including the pope in Rome. The Council took Pope John prisoner for defying them. The pope at Avignon, France exiled himself to a mountain in Spain.

Oddly, in 1415 while the Council of Constance was meeting to depose various popes and appoint their own, it summoned Huss to come and supposedly to speak about the papacy. They wanted papal reform, but did not want to get rid of the papacy completely. So when Huss arrived, he was imprisoned. When the King of Bohemia objected, he was told promises were not binding to heretics.

Finally Europe was back to having one pope - Gregory XII. Shortly after, Gregory resigned, and shortly after that, he died. The church was, for the next two years, without any pope!

Two days after forcing Pope Gregory to resign, the Council ordered Huss to be burned at the stake. When chained, Huss declared, "My Lord Jesus Christ was bound with a harder chain than this for my sake, and why then should I be ashamed of this rusty one?"

When the kindling was piled up to his neck, he was asked to abdicate his teachings. He replied, "I never preached any doctrine of an evil tendency; and what I taught with my lips I now seal with my blood." When the fire was started he sang a hymn "with so loud and cheerful a voice that he was heard through all the cracklings of the combustibles, and the noise of the Multitude." [2]

The following year, Huss's friend, Jerome of Prague in Bohemia, was similarly martyred. Going to the place of execution he sang hymns. When he arrived, he prayed, then embraced the stake. When the executioner started to set fire to the kindling behind him, he said, "Come here, and kindle it before my eyes; for if I had been afraid of it, I had not come to this place." While the fire burned, he sang hymns. The last thing he said was, "This soul in flames I offer Christ, to Thee." [3]

In 1418, the officials of the church of Rome decided that anyone partaking of the Lord's Supper was required to fast at least one hour beforehand, eliminating both food and water.

ORDAINED FASTING BEFORE LORD'S SUPPER/MASS/EASTER

Also in 1418, inspired by Huss, John de Trocznow "Zisca" of Bohemia formed an army of 40,000 to defend his country on behalf of religious freedom. But his emperor died and another was opposed to such freedom, so fought Zisca's army. Yet, in 1421 Zisca destroyed all the Catholic monasteries. The following year, Zisca, a nickname for one-eyed, was struck in the other eye with an arrow. But he continued to lead his army blind.

This "holy war" was bad for both sides to participate in; but at least they fought as equals on the battlefield rather than toward defenseless citizens.

After showing his superiority over the armies of Bohemia, Hungary and Poland, he turned to actual Reformation. He forbade all prayers for the dead, images, sacerdotal vestments, fasts and festivals.

He was offered the crown of Bohemia but refused it. He died of plague in 1424 and the former king regained power.

Persecution of the Reformers raged. Thereupon, some of the Reformers went to the senate allowing such persecution, and speared them.

Pope Martin V then declared the entire Bohemian race must be exterminated, offering to everyone in Germany and nearby kingdoms full remission of all sins if they killed even one Bohemian protestant.

A merchant of Prague, who openly admired John Huss and his teachings, was arrested in Silesia and sentenced to execution. As his legs were bound with ropes to be dragged through the streets, he was given one last chance to recant. He replied, "I glory in the very thoughts of dying for the sake of

Christ." Thereupon he was dragged through the city and burned at the stake.

Prince Ferdinand of the Rhine sent his own troops throughout Bohemia to get rid of the protestants. He had a "hanging court." But often the protestants were not afforded even that. Later he was made emperor.

They killed an aged minister in his bed, robbed and murdered another, and shot a third while he was preaching at church. A schoolmaster they stripped naked, beat, and then stoned. Another protestant was forced to watch his daughters raped, then was tortured to death. A minister and his wife were tied together and burned. Another minister was hung on a cross beam and broiled to death. Another minister was covered alternately with ice and burning coals until he died. Some instances cannot be printed here because of their hideousness.

Another minister they spit on and sent through the gauntlet, beating him with twigs, fists, ropes, wires, cudgels. They tied him upside down until the blood came out of his mouth and nose. They hung him by his right arm until it was dislocated and then set it. They repeated it with his left arm. Burning papers were placed between his fingers and toes. He was tormented with red-hot pinchers and put on the rack. They pulled out his fingernails and toenails. They slit his ears and nose, dragged him through the streets, and pulled out his teeth. Boiling lead was poured on his fingers and toes. He endured other things that are not repeatable here. One such torture killed him.

Twenty royal protestant sympathizers were sentenced to death in Prague, most of them tortured briefly and then beheaded. "The prisoners left the castle with as much cheerfulness as if they had been going to an agreeable entertainment, instead of a Violent death."

This is what some of them said before their deaths:

LORD SCHILIK, AGE 50: "I have God's favor, which is sufficient to inspire anyone with courage: the fear of death does not trouble me." LORD VISCUNT WINCESLAUS, AGE 70: "The Lord hath given, and the Lord hath taken away....the greater honor now attends ye, a crown of martyrdom is your portion."

LORD HARANT: "Almighty God! Forgive them, for they know not what they do." LORD HENRY OTTO: "I feel my spirits revived; God be praised for affording me such comfort."

EARL OF RUGENIA: "I am better pleased at the sentence of death, than if the emperor had given me life; for I find that it pleases God to have his truth defended, not by our swords, but by our blood. I shall now be speedily with Christ." SIR GASPAR KAPLITZ, AGE 86: "God reserved me until these years to be a spectacle to the world, and a sacrifice to himself....I will ask pardon of God, whom I have frequently offended; but not of the emperor, to whom I never gave any offense." DIONYSIUS SERVIUS, AGE 56: "They may destroy my body, but cannot injure my soul that I commend to my Redeemer." TOBIAS STEFFICK: "I have received during the whole course of my life, many favors from God; ought I not therefore cheerfully to take one bitter cup, when He thinks proper to present it?"

CHRISTOPHER CHOBER: "I come in the name of God, to die for His glory; I have fought the good fight, and finished my course; so, executioner, do your office." JOHN SHULTIS: "The righteous seem to die in the eyes of fools, but they only go to rest. Lord Jesus! ....Behold I am come; look on me, pity me, pardon my sins, and receive my soul."

MAXIMILIAN HOSTIALICK: "Lord, thou lettest Thou Thy servant depart in peace, according to Thy word; For mine eyes have seen Thy salvation." JOHN KUTNAUR: [To a priest trying to get him to recant] "Your superstitious faith I abhor, it leads to perdition, and I wish for no other arms against the terrors of death than a good conscience." SIMEON SUSSICKEY: "Every moment delays me from entering into the Kingdom of Christ." [4]

Around 1430, Nicholas of Cusa wrote that the pope was not infallible, but the church was; therefore, whenever the church was represented by the Council, the Council's decisions were infallible. The pope was just one member of the Council, therefore only got one vote.

In 1436, the Council of Constance, condemned clergy who had mistresses, changed parts of the liturgy, abolished some of the taxes to the pope, made new regulations for electing the pope.

Also, in an act of conciliation, during this time they allowed the followers of Huss to rejoin their reformed Catholic church.

However, the same year, many of Huss's followers merged with some Waldensians from Moravia to form the United Brethren, or sometimes called the Moravian Brethren.

In 1438 King Charles VII of France called his own Council that declared the pope could not decide on use of non-church property and they could nullify any French church nominee of the pope.

Also another all-church Council was called in Basle, Italy. Among other things, Pope Eugenius was deposed; but he refused to step down. They named Felix V as their pope, so once again the church had two popes for the next nine years. Felix's followers were in Switzerland, Austria, Bavaria, and Paris. France and Germany refused to choose sides.

But the Council made a serious mistake when it began granting indulgences in order to raise money to support itself. Therefore, most people - including French and Germans - went back to supporting the Pope Eugenius in Rome. After that, support for any Council began a fast decline and by 1449 the Conciliary Movement was over.

BIBLE BEGAN TO BE PRINTED WITH MOVABLE TYPE. At this time there were 33 translations of the Bible into various languages.

Beginning with Pope Nicholas V in 1447, attention was diverted to rediscovery of classical Rome and trying to recreate it. Nicholas added new wings onto the Vatican Palace and began the Vatican library.

His successor Calixtus III appointed two nephews as cardinals, one was only age 25. His successor, Pius II, openly bragged on his methods to seduce women. He had at least two illegitimate children. His successor Paul II had many concubines in the papal palace. He also started the papal publishing house.

ITALIAN TRANSLATION OF THE BIBLE: In 1471, Nixccolo Malermi translated the Bible into Italian from the Latin translation. It was printed in Venice.

CZECH TRANSLATION OF THE BIBLE: In 1475, the Bible was translated into the Czech language from the Latin, and printed with the new printing press.

FINNISH TRANSLATION OF THE BIBLE: M. Agricola translated the New Testament from the original Greek in the common language of his people.

Pope Sixtus IV, made at least six of his nephews cardinals, and gave another nephew four bishoprics and cardinal office all at the same time. He gave Giovanni de Medici (later Leo X) a church office at age 7, made him an abbot at age 8, and two more by the age of 12. Sixtus also built the Sistine Chapel in 1483.

In 1476, the church decided that the righteous dead could never leave purgatory and move on to heaven because they had not paid the penalty for their sins. Therefore, relatives of the dead were required to pay indulgences to get their loved ones out of purgatory.

ORDAINED INDULGENCES TO LEAVE PURGATORY

In 1477, the Roman church decided that Mary was the Spiritual Mother of all mankind.

ORDAINED MARY SPIRITUAL MOTHER OF MANKIND

DUTCH TRANSLATION OF THE BIBLE: That same year, the Delft Bible was translated from Latin into the language of the common people, but it was only the Old Testament.

ITALIAN TRANSLATION OF THE BIBLE: Bonifacio Ferrer made the Catalan translation from the Latin translation. It was later destroyed in the inquisition in 1498. Only a few fragments remain today.

Pope Innocent VIII had 16 children by various married women which he openly acknowledged and which he put into church offices. Previous popes had called their children nieces and nephews. He made his son by a previous marriage, Giovanni, a cardinal at age 12.

With building projects and supporting family members in church offices, there was a need for more money. More and more church offices were sold to the highest bidder. Pope Innocent pawned the papal triple tiara to line his pockets. A ring of cardinals forged papal decrees to sell on the market for hefty sums.

At Innocent's death, Alexander VI, who had tried unsuccessfully to be made pope previously, succeeded this time by offering the most money. As cardinal, he had several mistresses, one of whom bore him four children.

In 1489 he took a 13-year-old as a mistress and she bore him two more sons. He made her brother a cardinal and one of his sons a cardinal at age 18. Selling church office got so bad that the French threatened him. So Pope Alexander went to the Turkish sultan, a Muslim, for assistance.

In 1480, in reaction to the protestant Reformation, the Catholics entered into their own reformation, carried out by the Inquisitions as to who were true Catholics. The most infamous one was the Spanish Inquisition. It was about this time that Spanish King Ferdinand and Queen Isabella financed Columbus who thereupon discovered America.

Around 1494, a monk named Girolamo Savonarola began preaching about morals of both the people and the church leaders. Pope Alexander VI unsuccessfully tried to shut his meddling up by offering him a cardinal position. The following year Alexander ordered him to stop preaching. By 1497 Savonarola boldly attacked corruption in the church, so Alexander excommunicated him. The latter retorted that Alexander was not only a false pope, but not even a Christian.

The next year, some of his political enemies had Girolamo arrested. He was tortured 14 separate times, and later hung with two of his followers.

In 1495, the church introduced use of the rosary beads in prayer, each one representing one "Hail Mary" or whatever was designated.

INTRODUCED ROSARY

NOT WIDELY ACCEPTED

Also about this time, choirs were introduced into the church. They had to be men, and always were monks.

INTRODUCED CHOIRS

In the meantime, Pope Alexander's son by an earlier mistress was being groomed to be the next pope, but he was murdered in 1497. So the son of his youngest mistress made friends with the French who helped him grab land in northern Italy from other church office holders in the family. Once, for diversion, he turned some criminals loose in a courtyard of the Vatican and shot them from a window. But, when his father died, rather than be appointed pope, he became a mercenary soldier in Spain.

CZECH TRANSLATION OF THE BIBLE: About this time, John Huss translated the Bible into the language of his people. Actually he revised earlier Czech versions and modernized the antiquated language.

SLAVONIC TRANSLATION OF THE BIBLE: In 1499, Gennadius gathered together translations of various books of the Bible into one volume. They had all been translated from the Hebrew, Greek and Latin.

16th Century

Because of the edict of King Edward III of England a century earlier, persecution of Lollards (followers of Wyclif who called themselves the church of Christ) continued. In 1506 William Tilfrey was burned at the stake at Amersham. In 1507 Thomas Norris was burned for telling others of the Gospel.

In 1508, Lawrence Guale was burned at Salisbury for denying the real presence of Jesus in the bread and wine. A pious woman at Chippen Sudburne was burned. In 1511, William Succling and John Bannister were burned in Smithfield. In 1517 John Brown at Ashford was burned, first his feet to the bone, then the rest of him. Richard Hunn was killed in "Lollard's Tower" in the palace of Lambeth.

Pope Julius II had his own armies which he often personally led into France or Spain to retake lands formerly owned by the church. He also sponsored Michelangelo and laid the cornerstone for the new St. Peter's cathedral. In 1509 he marched on Venice and then northern Italy where the French were.

His successor was Leo X who had been made an archbishop at 8, a cardinal at 13, and held 27 different church offices before he was 13. He appointed cardinals as young as age 7. He and his cardinals vied with royalty throughout Europe for the luxury of their palaces and possessions.

In 1516, Dutchman Desiderius Erasmus, after spending years studying the writings of the apostles and early church fathers, printed for popular access a parallel New Testament in Greek and Latin. He dedicated it to Pope Leo X.

However, later Erasmus challenged the superstition of saints' relics, pilgrimages, and empty rituals. Although he believed in quiet study of the Scripture, he never broke from the Roman church.

By now, most of the clergy were taking their pay, but not showing up for work. Some even held more than one position and got paid for all of them. Many of the upper clergy were just sons of noblemen who needed a job, so were made bishop. Many of the parish priests were simply peasants who were willing to work for a penance even though they could not read enough Latin to do a complete mass. In Germany, only about seven percent of the parishes had a resident priest.

In 1517, Pope Leo X needed more money to build St. Peter's Basilica in Rome and the German archbishop needed enough money to repay himself for what it cost to buy his position. The two agreed on a special papal indulgence that would give the purchaser complete forgiveness of sins.

Martin Luther posted ninety-five theses on the castle church door in Wittenberg, the university bulletin board, challenging primarily the Roman church's entire system of salvation. He also admitted that some of John Huss' views were correct.

In 1520, Pope Leo condemned 41 Lutheran errors and condemned Luther as a heretic.

Luther kept emphasizing the priesthood of all believers, and wrote, "*The Babylonian Captivity of the church,*" wherein he attacked the seven sacraments of the Catholic church, declaring there were only two sacraments - baptism and the Lord's Supper. He also preached and *wrote that, even though "faith without works is dead," quoting Jesus' brother James, we are actually "saved by grace", quoting the apostle Paul.*

When Luther was pressured by Emperor Charles V of Germany to recant, he said his views were faithful to the Holy Scriptures and he would not recant. However, Prince Frederick of Saxony supported and protected him. Living relatively quiet, he ended his celibacy in 1525 and married a former nun, Katie. They had six children.

Gradually the Scandinavian kings of Denmark, Sweden and Norway adopted Luther's positions, as did many German princes. In 1529, when Emperor Charles in Germany tried to remove religious privileges of those agreeing with Luther, they protested. Thus began the term PROTESTANT.

ENGLISH TRANSLATION OF THE BIBLE: In 1522, William Tyndale began releasing his translation of the Bible from the original Greek rather than the Latin as his English predecessors had done. He did all of the New Testament. Part of the Old Testament he never finished. He released the entire New Testament in 1526.

Under the century-old edict of the King of England, more Lollards — followers of Wyclif who called themselves the church of Christ — were persecuted. In 1518 John Stilincen was burned at the stake in Smithfield. In 1519, Thomas Mann was burned at London. Robert Celin, for speaking against image worship and pilgrimages, was also burned. Also, James Brewster of Colchester was burned, and Christopher was burned at Newbury that same year. Then Robert Silks of Coventry was burned alive.

Meanwhile, in Switzerland in 1517, Ulrich Zwingli, a priest who had difficulty keeping his celibate vows, began studying the Scriptures more and more.

Zwingli began expository preaching, meaning that he chose a topic and exposed all the facts on it he could from the Scriptures. He realized the church of the New Testament was not the church of his day. The following year he attacked a local papal indulgence seller. At this time he also learned of Luther and his beliefs.

Challenged by the orthodox Roman Catholics, Zwingli took the matter to the town Council of Zurich. They agreed to let him continue to preach the gospel and the Scriptures. His teachings were so strong that the last Catholic mass was held in Zurich in

1525. protestant communion services took their place, but only four times a year.

FRENCH TRANSLATION OF THE BIBLE: In 1523, Jacques Lefevre translated the New Testament from Latin to the language of the common people. In 1530 he released the Old Testament. He was Catholic.

In 1524 in France, John Clark, an Albigense, nailed an announcement to the church door calling the pope Antichrist. **As a result he was repeatedly whipped and then branded on the forehead. Going to another city, he destroyed some images, for which he had his right ear and nose cut off. During further torture he sang the 150th Psalm forbidding idolatry. Then he was thrown into a fire and burned.**

Another French Albigense from Malda said that mass was a denial of the death and passion of Christ **and was burned by slow fire. John de Cadurco who also preached reformation in the church, was also burned at the stake.**

To escape persecution in France, many Waldense protestants fled to Italy and settled in the valleys of Piedmont. But they refused to make offerings for the dead in purgatory, did not go to mass, and did not confess their sins to the priest. Thus, the persecution began there.

At Turin, one man had his bowels taken out and put in a basin for him to look at until he died. At Revel, Catelin Girard was burned at the stake, but not before he declared, "When it is in the power of a man to eat and digest this solid stone, the religion for which I am about to suffer shall have an end, and not before." [5]

After a brief period of peace, another persecution arose in the same area when the Waldenses decided to preach the Gospel in public. Those captured were either skinned or burned alive.

GERMAN TRANSLATION OF THE BIBLE: Martin Luther translated the New Testament from the original Greek and published it in 1526. In 1534 he translated the Old Testament from the original Hebrew.

In 1526, Felix Mantz was thrown into prison in Switzerland for his beliefs in baptism. **On January 5, 1527, he was taken onto a boat, bound, and thrown into a river and drowned.** A hymn he wrote while awaiting his fate is in part as follows:

> *With rapture I will sing,*
> *Grateful to God for breath,*
> *The strong, almighty King*
> *Who saves my soul from death....*

Michael Sattler, was imprisoned in Strasburg, Switzerland, May 21, 1527. His tongue was torn out, his body tortured with hot tongs, then he was burned to death. But before his death, he penned this hymn in part:

> *Of such a man fear not the will,*
> *The body only he can kill.*

That same year in Munich, Germany, George Wagner was sentenced to be burned at the stake for his beliefs in baptism. Before his execution, he wrote this hymn, in part:

> *We praise our Father, God;*
> *To him hosannas bring.*

Carius Binder, who had been baptized and identified himself with the "Brethren," wrote this:

> *With all our hearts we thank thee,*
> *Thou holy one and true.*

Then on October 25, he and 38 others who believed in baptism were shut up in a house that was set on fire, and they all perished in the flames.

Leonhart Schiemer was baptized, then preached in Austria and Bavaria. He penned this hymn:

> *Thine holy place they have destroyed, Thine altars overthrown,*
> *And reaching forth their bloody hands, have foully slain thine own.*
> *And we alone, thy little flock – the few who still remain,*
> *Are exiles wandering through the land, in sorrow and in pain.*
>
> *We wander in the forests dark, with dogs upon our track;*
> *And like the captive, silent lamb, men bring us, prisoners, back.*

They point to us amid the throng, and with their taunts offend;
And long to let the sharpened axe on heretics descend.

In Tyrol, Bavaria, he was arrested and sentenced to death. On January 14, 1528, he was beheaded and burned.

In 1526, Hans Schlaffer in Germany discontinued his priesthood and was baptized by immersion. He then preached to others his opposition to infant baptism saying it was never commanded in the Scriptures. **The following year he was arrested.** He penned this hymn in part:

But Jesus Christ has died, and satisfied
The guilt that was mine own.

Early the following year he and 20 others of like faith were beheaded at Schwatz.

John Leopold, a tailor in Augsburg, was arrested for his beliefs in baptism. He wrote this hymn:

My God, thee will I praise
When my last hour shall come,
And them my voice I'll raise.
Within the heavenly home.
O Lord, most merciful and king,
Now strengthen my weak faith,
And give me peace of mind.

On April 25, 1528, he was executed for his beliefs.

Hans Hut was baptized in Augsburg, Germany, and associated with the Brethren. He preached in Silesia, Moravia and Austria. **He was imprisoned in Augsburg** and there wrote this hymn:

He points us to his holy word,
His Testament, in which the Lord
Appears our nature wearing....
Beneath his feet grim death hath trod,,
With truth himself arraying,
His mighty power displaying,
And all our fears allaying.

King James V of Scotland died, leaving a six-month-old daughter, Mary, Queen of Scots. While a child, the Catholics ruled, so Mary was raised Catholic.

Patrick Hamilton announced before the archbishop of St. Andrews that he disapproved of pilgrimages, purgatory, prayers to saints and for the dead. **Even while being burned at the stake, friars called out, "Turn, thou heretic; call upon our Lady."** He replied to one of them, "Wicked man, God forgive thee." In February 1528, he became Scotland's first protestant martyr. **A monk, Henry Forest, was murdered because he thought this was too harsh.**

DANISH TRANSLATION OF THE BIBLE: Christiern Pedersen translated the New Testament from two different Latin versions and Luther's German version into the language of his people.

SWISS TRANSLATION OF THE BIBLE: Put together by Huldreich Zwingli, it was called the Zurcher Bible. The New Testament was translated into the language of the common people from Luther's German translation in 1529. Later the Old Testament was completed.

In 1529 a protestant preacher was executed and war threatened between the protestants and Catholics. That same year, Luther and Zwingli met and agreed on all of their beliefs except the Lord's Supper. Luther continued to insist the bread and wine became Jesus' physical body, while Zwingli said it was just a memorial. In 1531 war did break out between the Catholics and protestants, and Zwingli with his troops were killed.

Ludwig Hetzer was baptized in 1523 and preached in various locations until exiled, so moved on. He also translated the Old Testament into German. Among several hymns written by him was this:

> *Fret not thyself, O pious heart,*
> *Though evil men surround thee.*

Finally, in Bischolszell, Switzerland, he was arrested and sentenced to death. On February 3, 1529, he was beheaded.

George Blaurock, a former monk, was baptized in 1525 and associated with the Brethren. Amidst his preaching, he wrote this hymn:

> Daily renew us and make us steadfast in persecution.
> Leave us not, thy children, from now on to the end.
> Extend to us thy fatherly hand, that we may finish our course.

In Tyrol, Switzerland, he was arrested, and burned at the stake in 1529. In reaction to the martyrdoms, that year, Urich Zwingli, a great Christian reform leader of Switzerland, wrote this hymn:

> *Lord, we cry to you for help. Only you can heal our pain.*
> *Out of deep distress we call. Help us, Lord, send peace again.*

These martyrdoms did not go unnoticed in Germany. At that time, Martin Luther wrote this hymn, trying to give courage:

> *A mighty fortress is our God, a Bulwark never failing;*
> *Our helper He, amid the flood of mortal ills prevailing.*
> *For still our ancient foe doth seek to work us woe;*
> *His craft and power are great, and armed with cruel hate,*
>   *On earth is not his equal.*
>
> *And tho this world, with evil filled, Should threaten to undo us;*
> *We will not fear, God hath willed His truth to triumph thru us.*
> *Let goods and kindred go, this mortal life also;*
> *The body they may kill: God's truth abideth still,*
>   *His kingdom is forever!*

In 1530, this hymn appeared among the Bohemian Brethren:

> *Now God be with us, for the night is closing;*
> *The light and darkness are of His disposing,*
> *And 'neath His shadow here to rest, we yield us,*
>   *For He will shield us.*

But still the persecutions continued by the mainline Roman church. In 1531, Martin Maler and six others were arrested in Schwabia, Germany, for preaching the Word,

especially about baptism. While there, Maler wrote this hymn in part:

> *In deep distress I cry to thee;*
> *My prayer, O God, attend.*

He was put on the rack and refused to recant. Thereupon he was executed.

Englishman, William Tyndale, tried to publish the New Testament in the common English of the people, but the Catholic bishop of London refused to allow it. So he went to the Continent where he printed his first edition in 1526. He spent the next decade trying to get his Bible to as many people as possible. **But he was finally arrested and burned at the stake in Brussels, Belgium, October 1536.**

In 1531 King Henry VIII, through an act of Parliament, officially separated England from the church in Rome. Now, as head of the church, he could annul his 15-year marriage to his brother's widow, claiming it had been incestuous because she was his sister-in-law. Besides, Catherine only gave him one daughter, Mary. He then married again, and Anne Boleyn bore him a girl, Elizabeth.

King Henry stopped all payments of money to the church at Rome and took them himself, and appointed all bishops. In 1535, anyone who disagreed was executed. The following year, frustrated that he still did not have a son, he drummed up charges of adultery on his current wife, had her executed, and married Jane Seymour who gave him a son, Edward.

The year after he permitted William Tyndale to be executed, he allowed an English translation of the Bible be openly available to the people. *By 1541 every parish was ordered to have an English Bible available for people to read.* Through the years as he changed his theological thinking, those who believed the opposite were executed.

DUTCH TRANSLATION OF THE BIBLE: In 1532 Luther's German Bible was translated into Dutch.

ITALIAN TRANSLATION OF THE BIBLE: That same year,

Antonio Brucioli translated the Bible into the language of the common people, using Erasmus' Latin version for the New Testament, and Pagninus' Latin version for the Old Testament.

HUNGARIAN TRANSLATION OF THE BIBLE: In 1533, the Pauline Epistles were translated from the Latin into the language of the common people.

GERMAN TRANSLATION OF THE BIBLE: In 1534 J. Dietenberger translated the Bible into the language of the people from the Latin. He also used Emser's New Testament and Luther's Old Testament. He was a Catholic.

FRENCH TRANSLATION OF THE BIBLE: In 1534, Olivetan translated the Bible into the language of his people from the Hebrew, Erasmus' Latin version, and Lefevre's New Testament.

FRENCH TRANSLATION OF THE BIBLE: In 1535, Olivetan translated the Bible into the language of his people from the Hebrew, Latin, and Lefevre's New Testament in French.

ENGLISH TRANSLATION OF THE BIBLE: That same year, Miles Coverdale translated the Bible into the language of the common people. Although German, he was hired by a German Lutheran merchant to do so because he did business in English. Copies of it were installed in many churches in England, and Queen Anne Boleyn had one in her chamber.

ENGLISH TRANSLATION OF THE BIBLE: Two years later in 1537, this Bible authorized by English monarchy, was a translation of Munster's Latin version of 1535 in the Old Testament and Erasmus' Latin version in the New Testament, the Swiss-German Zurich Bible, Luther's German Bible, and Tyndale's English version. Also much of it was lifted out of Coverdale's Bible. It became the direct ancestor of the Authorized Version, also known as the King James Version.

ENGLISH TRANSLATION OF THE BIBLE: In 1539, the Great Bible was translated into English and later edited by Coverdale. By royal injunction it was to be installed in every church. It was printed in Paris and nearly finished when the French inquisition intervened. Coverdale and his publisher fled with the types and printed sheets, and completed the printing in London in April 1539.

Worship Changes Since the First Century

WALDENSES TRANSLATION OF THE BIBLE: Although the Waldenses had had the New Testament and part of the Old printed in their language, they wanted the complete Bible. They furnished a Swiss printer with the entire Old and New Testament who accommodated them.

The Waldenses, the most powerful of the "heretics", refused as always to cooperate with the mainline Roman church, drew more and more converts, especially now with more translations of the Bible in the hands of the common people. They called themselves the church of Christ.

When further threatened by the pope, the Waldenses sent a message which in part said that they valued the King of kings, Jesus, who reigns in heaven, more than any earthly ruler, and their souls were more precious than their bodies.

Thereupon a minister, Jeffery Varnagle, was burned at the stake. Others were hanged, drowned, stabbed, pierced, thrown off cliffs, burned, crucified upside down, thrown to mad dogs, or racked to death. Those who could, escaped to the caves in the Alps.

Also in 1534 in Edinburgh, Scotland, David Stratton and Norman Gourlay were burned at the stake. A former dean of the Roman church, Thomas Forret, was also burned. Others burned to death were Killor and Beverage, a priest named Duncan Simson, and Robert Forrester.

About this time, Pope Paul III ascended the church throne and ordered the Waldenses persecuted anew.

The following hymns (in part) appeared in the Genevan Psalter:

> *Do not be silent, Lord God;*
> *The wicked speak against my life....*
> *You see, my Lord, how fearful, how spent I am,*
> *Like mere debris. Tormentors mock my frailty.*

In 1539 in Scotland, the archbishop condemned Jerome Russell and Alexander Kennedy (who was 18 years old) to be burned alive. On the way to their execution, Russell said, "The pain that we are to suffer is short, and shall be light; but our joy

and consolation shall never have end....Death cannot hurt us, for it is already destroyed by Him, for whose sake we are now going to suffer."

BETWEEN 1540 AND 1570, NEARLY ONE MILLION PROTESTANTS WERE PUT TO DEATH IN THE POPE'S WAR FOR THE EXTERMINATION OF THE WALDENSES.

One of their first was Bartholomew Hector, a bookseller of Turin, Italy, who was burned at the stake.

And in 1540, a man named Kugelmann wrote this hymn:

> *Out of the depths I cry, Lord. O Lord, please hear my call.*
> *Let your ears be attentive; I beg for mercy, Lord.*
> *O Lord, the enemy pursues me;*
> *My life lies broken where I've fallen.*
> *Let God arise and by his might*
> *Put all his enemies to flight*
> *With shame and consternation.*
> *For when the Lord God shall appear,*
> *he will consume, afar and near,*
> *With fire and desolation.*

HUNGARIAN TRANSLATION OF THE BIBLE: In 1541, J. Erdosi translated the New Testament from the original Greek into the language of the common people.

Some protestant Waldenses escaped to Venice, Italy, which, for some time, had left them alone in peace. But in 1542, persecution began there too.

This hymn appeared in the Genevan Psalter that year:

> *Pain and distress o'erwhelm me, I cry all night for mercy,*
> *My bed is wet with tears, my eyes can weep no longer;*
> *My enemies seem stronger, my awful foes and fears.*

Anthony Ricetti was sentenced to be drowned. His son begged him to become a Catholic instead, but his father replied, "A good Christian is bound to relinquish not only good and children, but life itself, for the glory of his Redeemer: therefore I am resolved to sacrifice everything in this transitory world, for the sake of salvation in a world that will last to eternity" [6]

The hierarchy offered to pay off the mortgage on his estate

if he became Catholic, but he still refused. **A few days later he was executed.**

Francis Spinola had written against claiming the bread and wine of the Lord's Supper were the actual body and blood of Christ. **He was imprisoned and executed.** "He went to meet death with the utmost serenity, seemed to wish for dissolution, and declaring that the prolongation of his life did but tend to retard that real happiness which could only be expected in the world to come."

Wolfgang Scuch, John Huglin, both ministers, and Leonard Keyser, a student, were burned at the stake. George Carpenter, a Bavarian, was hanged. [7]

SPANISH TRANSLATION OF THE BIBLE: In 1543, Enzinas Dryander translated the New Testament from the original Greek in the common language of his people.

About that same time, persecution arose in the Netherlands. The widow Wendelinuta was imprisoned. When a friend visited to tell her to at least keep her beliefs a secret, she replied, "You know not what you say; for with the heart we believe to righteousness, but with the tongue confession is made unto salvation." Soon after she was strangled and burned at the stake.

Two protestant ministers were burned at Colen. Nicholas in Antwerp was tied in a sack and drowned. Pistorius was burned at the stake. Seventeen protestants, including their minister, were beheaded in another Dutch village.

George Scherter, a minister of Salzburg, was beheaded and then burned. Percinal in Louviana was murdered in prison. Justus Insparg was beheaded for having Luther's sermons in his possession.

Giles Tilleman of Brussels was imprisoned and turned down a chance to escape in order to save punishment of his guards. When led to the stake he requested that most of the firewood be given to the poor. "A small quantity will suffice to consume me.

ENDNOTES

[1]. North, James B., *From Pentecost to the Present*, College Press, Joplin, MO, 1983, pg. 247

[2]. Forbush, William B., editor, *Fox's Book of Martyrs*, Zondervan Publishing House, 1968, pg. 143

[3]. Fox, pg. 146

[4]. Fox, pg. 154ff

[5]. Fox, pg. 94

[6]. Fox, pg. 101

[7]. Fox, pg. 102

BIBLIOGRAPHY

D'Aubigne, J. H. Merle, *History of the Reformation of the Sixteenth Century*, The Religious Tract Society, London, 1846

The Ecclesiastical History of Eusebius Pamphilus, Baker Book House, Grand Rapids, 1971

Encyclopedia Britannica, William Benton Publisher, Chicago, 1966

Forbush, William B., Editor, *Fox's Book of Martyrs*, Zondervan Publishing House, Grand Rapids, 1926

Goold, G. P., Editor, *Bede Historical Works: Ecclesiastical History of the English Nation*, Vol. I and II

Keyes, Nelson B., *Story of the Bible World*, Reader's Digest Assn,

Pleasantville, NY, 1962

Lightfoot, J.B., Editor, *The Apostolic Fathers,* Baker Book House, Grand Rapids, 1965

McDonald, William J., Editor, *The New Catholic Encyclopedia*, McGraw-Hill, Chicago, 1962

North, James B., *From Pentecost to the Present*, College Press Publishing, Joplin, Mo., 1983

Simon, Edith, *Great Ages of Man: The Reformation,* Time-Life Books, NY, 1968

Burrage, Henry S., *[Ana]Baptist Hymn Writers and their Hymns*, Brown Thurston & Co., Portland, Maine, 1889

Wells, H. G., *The Outline of History,* Garden City Books, NY, 1961

3. CHANGES IN WORSHIP

16th to 18th Centuries

16th Century (cont)

Back in Paris in 1534, Frenchman John Calvin had gone through a conversion "experience" that broke him away from the Roman church. The following year, while living briefly in Italy, he wrote *The Institutes of the Christian Religion* which is still referred to today. *He settled in Geneva, Switzerland, where he organized the church with four types of officers: Pastors who heard all cases of church discipline, elders who visited all families, deacons, and teachers.*

Through the next 30 years, he taught that everyone has been predestined by God whether they are to be saved or condemned, Jesus died only for the saved, people cannot resist the Spirit if they were called to be saved, it is impossible for anyone to fall from being saved or rise from being unsaved. Those who followed Calvin in various areas of Europe were called French Reformed, Dutch Reformed, German Reformed, Swiss Reformed, and Hungarian Reformed. Other organizations later accepted this teaching also, including Presbyterian and Baptist.

In 1547, to counter-attack the movement toward people reading the Bible for themselves and breaking away from the mainline Roman church despite hideous tortures and deaths, the Catholic Council of Trent was called. Many major decisions were made at this Council.

It was declared that the scripture and church tradition were equally valid sources of religious truth, and the Catholic church had the sole right to interpret the Scriptures.

ORDAINED CHURCH TRADITION AS
SACRED AS BIBLE
ORDAINED ONLY CATHOLIC CHURCH COULD INTERPRET

SCRIPTURE

They listed which books should be included in the Old and New Testament, including several that were not previously admitted and which today protestants still do not admit. This had already been done centuries earlier, but they made it official this time in an effort to regain control of the Scriptures which they now declared exclusively under the power of the Roman church.

ORDAINED OVER 70 BOOKS IN BIBLE

SEVERAL NOT ACCEPTED BY PROTESTANTS

They also declared the Latin translation from the Greek by Jerome in the fourth century was the only authorized text of scripture. They called it the Latin Vulgate. It had 2000 mistakes in it. Also, he translated all references to priests as *pontiffs*, and all references to high priests as *pontiffs maximus*.

ORDAINED JEROME'S LATIN BIBLE

They stated that Christ instituted seven sacraments. They also confirmed Transubstantiation — the bread and wine becoming the actual body and blood of Jesus — and they condemned the Lutheran, Calvinist, and Zwinglian doctrines of the Lord's Supper. They also said that mass (the Lord's Supper) was required to be said by the bishop in Latin.

ORDAINED BREAD & WINE ARE ACTUALLY JESUS
ORDAINED LORD'S SUPPER IN LATIN

They declared that babies inherit original sin, so must be baptized or end up in purgatory. They declared absolutely the existence of purgatory and described it.

ORDAINED ORIGINAL SIN & INFANT BAPTISM
ORDAINED EXISTENCE OF PURGATORY

Also, the term "minister" was to refer to anyone in the church who was a deacon or above. They reiterated and declared that all sins must be confessed in private to a priest. They also declared that all pastors must be ordained.

ORDAINED QUALIFICATIONS OF MINISTER
ORDAINED ALL SINS BE CONFESSED TO PRIEST
ORDAINED HOW PASTORS ARE TO BE ORDAINED

Further, by this time, all choir members were required to wear vestments. Gold was determined as the color where churches could not afford a variety. Otherwise, for ordinary worship, green was worn, white was used for Christmas and Easter, red for Pentecost, violet for lent, black for funerals.

ORDAINED CHOIR VESTMENTS

Then, for the next 100 years, Catholics and protestants (protesters to the Catholic church) clashed violently, always politically, and sometimes in war.

In 1545 Albigense Francis Bribard in France spoke in favor of reforming the Roman church and had his tongue cut out, then was burned. That same year James Cobard said mass was useless and absurd and so was burned at the stake. At Malda, 14 other men were burned for similar beliefs. In 1546, Peter Chapot brought a number of Bibles in the French language to France and sold them there. He was executed for it.

In 1549, Monsieur Blondel, an Albigense in Paris, was burned for his faith, as were 19-year-old Herbert in Dijon and Florent Venote, France.

Soon after, Louis Bourgeois set to music these hymns (in part):

> Protect me from the arrogant and proud;
> They scorn and laugh at those who seek your pleasure.
> Sometimes I am depressed and sad at heart;
> Revive my soul according to your precepts.

Worship Changes Since the First Century

> O Lord, my enemies rise up to conquer me;
> They shower me with taunting.
>
> Comfort, comfort now my people;
> Speak of peace: So says our God.
> Comfort those who sit in darkness [dungeons]
> Mourning under sorrow's load.
>
> *Lord, to you my soul is lifted. Let me never be ashamed*
> *That I trust in you to keep me, though I seem to wait in vain.*

Christians all over the world still today sing this next hymn of courage set to music by Bourgeois:

> All people that on earth do dwell,
> Sing to the Lord with cheerful voice.
> Serve him with joy, his praises tell,
> Come now before him and rejoice!

Also that year, another Frenchman, Claude Goudimel, wrote this hymn:

> Defend me, Lord, from those who charge me
> With shameful insults, lies, and slurs.
> Come, save your servant from evil ones.
>
> In you alone I can find refuge....
> Our faith seems in vain.
> All covered with darkness, to you we complain.

CZECH TRANSLATION OF THE BIBLE: Around 1550 Jan Blahoslav translated the New Testament into the language of his people. It was the basis of the later Bible of Kralice published in 1579.

DANISH TRANSLATION OF THE BIBLE: In 1550, J. Seklucyan published the New Testament in the language of his people from the original Greek. It was the first Polish Bible put out with the new printing press.

Back in 1547, King Henry of England had died and his 10-year-old son, Edward, had become king. *His uncle and guardian,*

Edward Seymour, ordered the mass be turned into a communion service in the common language. In 1553, Edward died and his oldest sister, Mary, became queen. Mary had been raised Catholic, so became a tool for the Roman church.

Under "Bloody Mary" in Great Britain thousands of protestants were put to death. In 1554 it included John Rogers, a close friend of William Tyndale and Miles Coverdale who both had translated the Bible into English, and a preacher, Lawrence Saunders.

In 1546 Martin Luther in Germany died. Then Charles V, the last Emperor of the "Holy Roman Empire" and King of Spain began a renewed campaign against the protestants in Germany, Spain, and Italy.

In Germany Henry Voes, John Esch and Henry Sutphen were burned at the stake. All protestants in Middleburg were killed by the sword, and those in Vienna burned at the stake.

Peter Spengler of Schalet was sentenced to execution for not going to mass, not making confession, and not believing the bread and wine because Jesus' actual body and blood. He encouraged those watching, sang a hymn, and was thrown into a river to drown.

A protestant man was encouraged to at least whisper his renunciation of Protestantism in the ears of the friar. He replied loudly, "Trouble me not, friar, I have confessed my sins to God, and obtained absolution through the merits of Jesus Christ. Let me not be pestered with these men, but perform your duty." Then he was beheaded. [1]

POLISH TRANSLATION OF THE BIBLE: In 1553, J. Seklucyan translated the New Testament into the language of his people from the original Greek.

Meanwhile, John Mollius had been raised in a monastery and prepared to become a priest. Having read the Scriptures in Latin, when he came across writings of the protestants, he saw they made sense, so began preaching against the Catholic church. He taught against original sin, infallibility of the church and pope, purgatory, mass, prayers for the dead in purgatory, prayers for saints, performing services in an unknown tongue and so on.

Persecution of protestant Waldenses in Italy had

continued. Now a declared protestant himself, Mollius was arrested, hung, and his body burned.

DUTCH TRANSLATION OF THE BIBLE: In 1554, the New Testament was translated into the language of the common people based on Erasmus' Greek text of the New Testament.

In 1554, two Albigenses in Niverne, France, were smeared with grease, brimstone, and gunpowder, their tongues cut out, and burned to death.

In 1555 in Italy, protestant Waldensian Algerius was arrested and sent to Rome where appeals were made to him to recant. When they saw it was no use, they burned him at the stake.

Queen Mary of England ("Bloody Mary"), a staunch Catholic, had the Parliament vote to return her country to the church of Rome. But the people refused to obey the bishops, so in 1555 the persecution rose to its heights. **One of the first, Bishop Latimer, said just before his burning, "Have faith, Master Ridley; today we shall light a fire which shall illuminate the world."**

Under this queen were burned at the stake John Hooper, former bishop; Dr. Rowland Taylor who refused to allow Easter mass; William Hunter who refused to go to mass; Robert Farrar for preaching against popish idolatry; Rowlands White for refusing to bow down to the host (bread of the Lord's Supper becoming Christ); George Marsh for preaching against the papacy; William Flower, a former monk and priest; John Cardmaker and John Warne for refusing to bow to idols.

In 1556, the burnings continued, mostly among protestant leaders, and numbered at least one hundred – an average of one every three days.

In 1557, Archbishop Parker rhymed the 23rd Psalm for singing as follows:

To feed my neede: he will me leade
To pastures green and fat:
He forth brought me: in libertie
To waters delicate.

Meanwhile, in Scotland, protestants continued to be

persecuted and executed. Back in 1546 the protestants had stormed the castle and killed the Catholic cardinal. Among the attackers was John Knox. Spending the next ten years in protestant England, he prayed, "Lord, give me Scotland or I die!"

By 1560 he had won over the Scottish to Protestantism. *The Scottish Parliament rejected papal authority, abolished the mass, withdrew authority of the bishops,* and adopted a confession of faith drawn up by Knox later to be known as the Westminster Confession, which organized the church into presbyteries. Thus was born the Presbyterian church.

In England in 1556, Archbishop Cranmer, who had translated parts of the Bible into English, read it in church, and openly sold copies. **He was burned at the stake, as were probably a hundred other leaders of the Reformation Movement.**

Meanwhile, in Italy in 1559, John Alloysius and James Bovellus were burned as heretics in Rome. In 1560 a young Englishman visiting Rome saw a bishop carry the bread of the Lord's Supper with pomp and ceremony. He grabbed it, threw it on the ground and stepped on it, declaring, "Ye wretched idolaters, who neglect the true God, to adore a morsel of bread."

Thereupon, the pope ordered that he be led naked through the streets of Rome with the image of the devil on his head, his right hand cut off, then burned. "At his place of executed he kissed the chains that were to bind him to the stake. A monk presenting the figure of a saint to him, he struck it aside." Then he was burned. [2]

SWISS TRANSLATION OF THE BIBLE: This Bible was translated in 1560 into the language of the common people, and published in Geneva.

UPPER ENGADINE TRANSLATION OF THE BIBLE: J. Bifrun translated the Bible from the Vulgate into this Romanish Swiss dialect in 1560.

In 1560, Pope Pius IV began persecuting Waldenses in the area of Calabria, Italy, for not being Roman Catholics and going to mass, not making their boys priests and girls nuns, and not bowing to images and going on pilgrimages.

Instead of giving in, the Waldenses fled to the forests

outside their cities. Many were hunted down and killed - men, women and children. Some were hung, some burned, some stabbed, and some were starved to death.

In one city, thirty who did not comply were put on the rack. Those who survived "boldly declared that no tortures of body, or terrors of mind, should ever induce them to renounce their God or worship images" [3]. In another city, sixty women were tortured on the rack where the ropes cut through their arms and legs to the bone and many died there.

Many of these were stripped naked and beaten to death with iron rods, stabbed, thrown off towers, or covered with pitch and burned alive. One monk personally cut the throats of 80 men, women and children, then quartered their bodies to be taken on stakes to nearby towns. The brutalities continued until they were satisfied all the protestant Waldenses had been exterminated.

POLISH TRANSLATION OF THE BIBLE: This Cracow Bible was the first entire Bible published in the language of the people, and was translated from the Latin in 1561.

RUMANIAN TRANSLATION OF THE BIBLE: Coresi translated the Acts of the Apostles from earlier manuscripts written during the Huss movement.

Amidst this, in 1562, this hymn appeared in the Genevan Psalter which is sung by many Christians even today:

> *Let us with a gladsome mind*
> *Praise the Lord, for he is kind.*
> *Sound again his name abroad,*
> *For of gods he is the God.*

WELSH TRANSLATION OF THE BIBLE: William Salesbury translated the New Testament from the original Greek into the common language of his people in 1567.

ENGLISH TRANSLATION OF THE BIBLE: The Bishop's Bible was published in 1568 in English.

In Antwerp, Netherlands, in 1568 Scoblant, Hues and Coomans were imprisoned. Prior to his execution, Hues declared, "I am now going to throw off this mantle of clay, to be clad in robes of eternal glory. I hope I may be the last martyr...that the church of Christ may have rest here, as his servants will hereafter." At the stake, he said the Lord's prayer and sang the Fortieth Psalm, then was burned.

SPANISH TRANSLATION OF THE BIBLE: C. de Reyna translated only the Old Testament from the Hebrew especially for Spanish-speaking Jews in 1569.

In 1570, the Roman church declared that the crucifix (cross with Jesus on it) was required to be on table of Lord's Supper, and that the chalice containing the wine to be held up during the ritual.

ORDAINED A CRUCIFIX MUST BE ON ALTAR

In 1572, the Roman church declared that all Christians must bow before the bread and wine of the Lord's Supper (mass).

ORDAINED BOWING TO AND WORSHIPPING BREAD AND WINE

In France between 1562 and 1595, the protestants - called Huguenots there - fought eight wars with the Catholics. The worst was St. Bartholomew's massacre of 1572 in which some 70,000 Huguenots were killed, even those in the palace who ran through its halls trying in vain to escape. Similar orders were sent to all the provinces of France, resulting in 100,000 protestants slaughtered for their faith.

During the peaceful reign of Bloody Mary's sister in England, Elizabeth, smaller groups of reformers arose here and on the mainland of Europe, some temporarily and others permanently. Those insisting on the leading of an inner light were called Spiritualists, though each group varied somewhat from the others.

The Evangelical Rationalists got involved with whether God was one or three. **One leader, Servetus, was burned at the stake in Geneva under order of protestant John Calvin and his**

Council. Sozzini went to Poland where he laid the foundation for the Unitarian church (which has more recently eliminated the New Testament as an authority). [Note: Later, a few protestant groups in America began to burn people at the stake, calling them heretics and witches.]

The most numerous groups, though, were Anabaptists whose major movement began in Switzerland under Zwingli. They did not believe in infant baptism, and rebaptized adults who were able to have faith and understanding. However, many practiced sprinkling and pouring. Many became known as the Swiss Brethren. They moved to the Netherlands, but were wiped out in a battle with the Catholics and Lutherans.

Menno Simons, a Dutchman whose brother died in that battle, gave direction to the remaining Anabaptists, and they became known as the Mennonites who, even today, learned their lesson and still refuse to take up arms.

In the 1580s, Robert Browne in England led a splinter group of Puritans called the English Baptists. Jacobus Arminius began the Arminians who disagreed with Calvin, and believed no one was predestined to be saved, Jesus died for everyone, and saints can fall from grace.

In 1559 the English Parliament voted to reinstitute the church of England. In 1563 the statement of doctrine called the Thirty-Nine Articles, strongly Calvinist in theology, was drawn up to represent the church of England.

In 1560, Nicholas Burton, an Englishman who sailed to Spain with many goods for sale, was imprisoned in order to illegally confiscate his goods. While there he explained the Word of God and converted the other. For this he was burned at the stake.

For similar reasons, Mark Brughes, an Englishman visiting Portugal, was burned at the stake. Sixteen-year-old William Hoker, also visiting Spain, was stoned to death in Seville.

In 1561, William Kethe set this still familiar poem to a tune written by Louis Bourgeois:

All people that on earth do dwell,

> *Sing to the Lord with cheerful voice;*
> *Him serve with fear, His praise forth tell;*
> *Come ye before Him and rejoice.*
>
> *For why? The Lord our God is good;*
> *His mercy is forever sure;*
> *His truth at all times firmly stood,*
> *And shall from age to age endure.*

In 1570 Pope Pius V excommunicated and deposed Queen Elizabeth of England, which she didn't care about anyway. Because so many practices were Roman Catholic, however, many later Anglican members called themselves the Anglo-Catholics. It would be another two centuries before they began to officially be called the Anglican church.

Those later known as Puritans wanted to "purify" the Anglican church further, especially doing away with garments worn by priests and preachers during service. Although they liked formal worship, they preferred the simple robes typical of the Calvinists.

In 1572, Joachim Magdeburg wrote this hymn:

> Who trusts in God, a strong abode in heaven and earth possesses;
> Who looks in love to Christ above, no fear his heart oppresses.
> In Thee alone, dear Lord, we owe sweet hope and consolation;
> Our shield from foes, balm for woes, great and sure salvation.

Also in 1572, King Charles IX of France decided to marry his sister, Margaret of Valois, to Henry of Navarre, son of the king of Navarre. **Two days after a grand wedding on a high platform in Paris, a massacre began of Huguenots, taking thousands of lives there and in nearby cities.**

Stories abound of people running through the streets only to meet their death anyway through stabbing, beheading, drowning, shooting, slow torture. One city was surrounded seven months and 18,000 inhabitants died by slow starvation. A total of 100,000 were killed around France.

In 1579, William Daman wrote this hymn:

> *O Lord, how many they who deeply trouble me;*
> *How greatly are they multiplied who do me injury.*

After the massacre, Henry of Navarre became the leader of the Huguenots. In 1589, after three kings had died without a son, Henry, a distant cousin of the king, inherited the throne. But Catholic Paris refused to accept him. Fighting continued four more years. Finally, in 1593, he converted to Catholicism, becoming King Henry IV.

Still, he was sympathetic to the Huguenots and gave them permission to worship whenever and where ever they wanted except in Paris, while also maintaining their civil and political rights. As a guarantee, he allowed them to have 200 fortified garrisons throughout France, supported by the king. This was called the Edict of Nantes. It lasted 100 years.

RUMANIAN TRANSLATION OF THE BIBLE: In 1582 the Old Testament was translated into the language of the common people who were Calvinists.

WELSH TRANSLATION OF THE BIBLE: In 1588, this Bible was translated by William Morgan into the language of his people. In some ways it was an offshoot of the Salesbury New Testament translated thirty years earlier. It is used today.

HUNGARIAN TRANSLATION OF THE BIBLE: In 1590, G. Karoli translated the Bible into the language of his people from the original Greek and Hebrew.

In 1592, rejoicing in the triumphs of Christianity, this well-known Christmas hymn was written by T. Este:

> *While shepherds watched their flocks by night,*
> *All seated on the ground,*
> *An angel of the Lord came down,*
> *And glory shone around.*

17th Century

Early in this century, David Dickson in Scotland wrote this hymn:

> *O Mother dear, Jerusalem!*

When shall I come to thee?
When shall my sorrows have an end?
Thy joys when shall I see?

O happy harbor of the saints!
O sweet and pleasant soil!
In thee no sorrow may be found,
No grief, no care, no toil.

In 1600, Pope Clement VIII tried to bribe the protestants in Italy to become Catholics. He also offered rewards to anyone witnessing them committing a crime. Nothing stopped them.

Among many others, Sebastian Basan was imprisoned, tortured for 15 months, then burned at the stake.

With the death of Mary Queen of Scots in 1587, and Queen Elizabeth of England in 1603, James VI became King of both countries, thus joining the monarchy until this death.

In 1604 when the Puritans wanted to reduce the power of bishops, King James refused. But at the same conference, he approved an authorized English translation of the Bible. It contained these introductory words....

"To the most high and mighty prince, James, by the Grace of God, King of Great Britain, France, and Ireland, defender of the faith. The translators of the Bible wish Grace, Mercy, and Peace, through Jesus Christ our Lord....

"Among all our joys, there was no one that more filled our hearts, than the blessed continuance of the preaching of God's sacred Word among us....manifesting itself abroad in the farthest parts of Christendom, by writing in defense of the Truth, (which hath given such a blow unto that man of sin, as will not be healed)....

"There are infinite arguments of this right christian and religious affection in Your Majesty; but none is more forcible to declare it to others than the vehement and perpetuated desire of accomplishing and publishing of this work....Things of this quality have ever been subject to the censures of ill-meaning and discontented persons....

"So that if, on the one side, we shall be traduced by Popish Persons at home or abroad, who therefore will malign us, because we are poor instruments to make God's holy Truth to be yet more and more known unto the people, whom they desire still to keep in ignorance and darkness; or if, on the other side, we shall be maligned by self-conceited Brethren, who run their own ways, and give liking unto nothing, but what is framed by themselves, and hammered on their anvil....

"We may rest secure, supported within by the truth and innocency of a good conscience, having walked the ways of simplicity and integrity...which will ever give countenance to honest and Christian endeavours against bitter censures." [4]

DANISH TRANSLATION OF THE BIBLE: In 1607, Hans Poulsen Resent translated the Bible from the original Greek and Hebrew into Danish.

ITALIAN TRANSLATION OF THE BIBLE: That same year, Giovanni Diodati published this Bible in the language of the common people. It was used in Geneva for the protestants.

ENGLISH TRANSLATION OF THE BIBLE: Not able to fight the tide of translations into the language of the common people, between 1582 and 1610, the Catholic church commissioned this Reims-Douai translation and became its official English Version. Still used today, it is usually called the Douai version.

ENGLISH TRANSLATION OF THE BIBLE: Under the authority of King James, 54 scholars were assembled and translated the version that would be officially authorized for use in all churches in England. It was published in 1611.

The Roman church decided about this time that candles must always be used in connection with the Lord Supper, the mass.

ORDAINED CANDLES AT MASS [LORD'S SUPPER]

In 1620, persecution of the Albigenses in France became severe; also in Germany in 1630. Tortures like those already mentioned were repeated on thousands of people. Finally Great Britain intervened and the persecutions stopped for awhile.

In 1623, John Milton wrote this hymn:

Let us with a gladsome mind
Praise the Lord, for He is kind;
For His mercies aye endure,
Ever faithful, ever sure.

And in 1625, this famous Thanksgiving hymn appeared in the Netherlands, written by A. Valerius:

We gather together to ask the Lord's blessing;
He chastens and hastens His will to make known;
The wicked oppressing now cease from distressing;

Sing praises to His name; He forgets not His own.

England and Scotland continued to vacillate between Protestantism and Catholicism. William Laud was made Catholic Archbishop of Canterbury in 1633. He was so anti-Puritan that he began an Inquisition aimed directly at the Puritans.

During this time, Johann Heerman wrote this hymn:

> *When dangers gather round,*
> *O keep me calm and fearless;*
> *Help me to bear the cross*
> *When life seems dark and cheerless.*

But with the government back in Puritan hands under Oliver Cromwell, the Scottish parliament eliminated government of the church by bishops, and adopted the Westminster Confession of Faith, the Larger Catechism and Shorter Catechisms, three documents on which the Presbyterian church rely even today.

In 1636, Martin Rinkart wrote this well-known hymn:

> *Now thank we all our God with heart and hands and voices,*
> *Who wondrous things has done, in whom his world rejoices.*

But persecution was still far from over, and in 1641, George Neumark of Germany wrote this hymn:

> *What can these anxious cares avail thee,*
> *These never-ceasing moans and sighs?*
> *What can it help, if thou bewail thee*
> *O'er each dark moment as it flies?*
> *Our cross and trials do but press*
> *The heavier for our bitterness.*

FINNISH TRANSLATION OF THE BIBLE: In 1642, the Bible was translated into the language of the common people from the original Greek and Hebrew.

In 1644, Matthaus A. von Lowenstern wrote this hymn:

> *Lord, Thou cans't help when earthly armor faileth;*
> *Lord, Thou canst save when sin itself assaileth;*

Worship Changes Since the First Century

Christ, o'er Thy Rock nor death nor hell prevaileth;
Grant us Thy peace, Lord.

DANISH TRANSLATION OF THE BIBLE: In 1647, the Bible was translated into the language of the common people, being an updated revision of Resen's earlier edition.

RUMANIAN TRANSLATION OF THE BIBLE: In 1648, Simion Stefan published the Four Gospels in parallel with Greek, Latin, and Slavonic.

1648 heavy persecution raged throughout Lithuania and Poland. Among them was Adrian Chalinski who was put close enough to a fire to singe him, and was slowly roasted alive.

In 1653, Johann Cruger wrote this hymn:

The foes who hate me unprovoked are strong and still increase,
Though to disarm their enmity my right I yield for peace.

In January 1655 in the Piedmont Valleys of Italy, the church ordered confiscation of all property of anyone who did not return to the Catholic church within three days. The protesters fled into the Alps. They were pursued by troops. Following is an account of just a few of the deaths.

In one village they beheaded 150 women and beat the children to death. Protesters in Vilario and Bobbio refusing to go to mass above age 15 were crucified upside down, and those under that age were strangled. Sarah Rastignole des Vignes, age 60, refused to pray to a saint so was stabbed with a sickle, then beheaded.

A man in Thrassiniere had swords run into his ears and through his feet, his fingernails and toenails were torn off. He was dragged through the street, then strangled with a rope.

A woman named Armand, had her arms and legs cut off. Two old women were stabbed and left for dead. A very old woman had her nose and hands cut off and left to die. Magdalen Bertino was stripped naked, her head tied between her legs, and thrown off a cliff. Mary Raymondet was skinned alive. Magdalen Pilot of Vilario was cut up in a cave of Castolus. Ann Charboniere had a stake thrust up her body and was left to die.

Jacob and David Perrin, elders of the church in Vilario, were skinned. Giovanni Rostagnal, 80 years old, had his nose and ears cut off, then was skinned. Seven others had their mouths stuffed with gunpowder and set on fire.

Jacob Birone of Rorata was stripped naked, had his fingernails and toenails torn off, holes bored through his hands, led through the streets being bludgeoned on the way. He constantly refused when asked, "Will you go to mass? Will you go to mass?" So they beheaded him.

Paul Garnier's eyes were put out, then he was skinned alive. Historian Fox reports "he bore all his sufferings with the most exemplary patience, praised God as long as he could speak." [5]

Daniel Cardon of Rocappiata was beheaded. Two old blind women of St. Giovanni were burned. A widow and her daughter of La Torre, were stoned. Paul Giles had his neck shot, nose and chin slit, then was stabbed.

Eleven men of Garcigliana were forced to push each other into a furnace. Michael Gonet, 90 years old, was burned, and Baptista Oudri, also old, was stabbed. Tormenters drew ropes through the heels of Frasche Bartholomew, dragged him to prison with them, then he died.

Cypriania Bustia, refusing to turn Catholic, said, "I would rather renounce life, or turn dog." When Jacob Roseno refused to pray to the saints, soldiers beat him and shot him, but still he cried out his refusal. He was then beheaded.

Paul Clement, an elder of the church in Rossana, was shown the recently executed bodies of other protestants. He replied, "You may kill the body, but you cannot prejudice the soul of a true believer." He was ordered hung.

Daniel Rambaut of Vilario was arrested and refused to believe the Catholic doctrine, which someone put in writing. It is reported in *Fox's Book of Martyrs* in part, as follows:

"To believe the real presence [of Jesus] in the host [bread] is a shocking union of both blasphemy and idolatry. That fancy words...by converting the wafer and wine into the real and identical body and blood of Christ, which was crucified and which afterward ascended into heaven, is too gross an absurdity for even a child to believe...nothing but blind

superstition could make the Roman Catholics put a confidence in anything so completely ridiculous....

"The doctrine of purgatory was more consistent and absurd than a fairy tale....the pope's being infallible was an impossibility, and the pope arrogantly laid claim to what could belong to God only....saying masses for the dead was ridiculous...as the fate of all is finally decided on the departure of the soul from the body...praying to saints for the remission of sins is misplacing adoration....God only can pardon our errors."

Thereupon, one finger was cut off every day, then every toe, then daily a hand and a foot. "But finding that he bore his sufferings with the most admirable patience, increased both in fortitude and resignation, and maintained his faith with steadfast resolution and unshaken constancy, they stabbed him to the heart." [6]

Numerous others were thusly tortured and murdered for protesting and wanting to follow only the Bible.

In mid-century Paulus Gerhardt of Saxony, Germany, a follower of Luther, was caught between the beliefs of Luther, Calvin, and the Catholic church and alternately persecuted by one of the groups. He began writing his hymns at the end of the Thirty Years' War. Among his 120 hymns he wrote were these written in 1653:

>*Give to the winds your fears in hope be undismayed;*
>*God hears your sighs and counts your tears,*
>*God shall lift up your head.*

In 1657, Australian Johann Scheffler wrote this hymn:

>*Thee will I love, my strength, my tower;*
>*Thee will I love my joy, my crown....*
>*Uphold me in the doubtful race,*
>*Nor suffer me again to stray;*
>*Strengthen my feet with steady pace*
>*Still to press forward in Thy way.*

ARMENIAN TRANSLATION OF THE BIBLE: In 1666, Oskan of Yerevan translated the Bible into the language of his people and had it printed in Amsterdam.

FRENCH TRANSLATION OF THE BIBLE: The following year in 1667, Isaac Louis de Sacy translated the Bible into the language of his people from the Latin. He was Catholic.

In 1674, an Englishman named Thomas Ken, who would alternately grow in and out of favor with various kings of England over a period of 40 years, wrote this still-familiar hymn:

> *Praise God from whom all blessings flow,*
> *Praise Him all creatures here below;*
> *Praise Him above, ye heavenly hosts,*
> *Praise Father, Son and Holy Ghost.*

In 1666, French King Louis XIV, a Catholic king, came to power and stripped the Huguenots of every favor provided them by King Henry. He enacted sixty clauses by which Huguenots could legally be persecuted. The government closed their hospitals, schools, and colleges, and many of their church buildings.

Many Huguenot children were abducted and raised as Catholics. He executed thousands of Huguenots on the gallows for resisting Catholic conversions. Ministers were exiled, but the people were forbidden to leave the country. Yet 250,000 managed to escape.

In 1685 in France, the peace Edict of Nantes with the Huguenots was revoked and the persecution started once more. protestants (Huguenots) were expelled from all offices and employments, children age 7 and above were taken away to be raised Catholic, all were forbidden to meet for religious purposes, and passage out of the country was denied.

Soldiers entered cities and announced, "Die, or be Catholics!" They were led by bishops, and urged on by monks among them. Some Huguenots were tortured with smoke while hanging upside down, others had their hair plucked out one strand at a time, their bodies were used as pincushions, or dragged by the nose. Women and children who still refused to become Catholic were imprisoned in monasteries, and the men were put in dungeons for perpetual torture.

Still about 150,000 escaped to other countries.

Worship Changes Since the First Century

Over in Germany, which was receiving many fleeing persecution in Western Europe, Johannes Olearius wrote this hymn of comfort in 1671:

> *Comfort, comfort ye My people,*
> *Speak ye peace, thus saith our God.*

And in 1677 this famous German hymn of unknown origin appeared to bring peace to aching Christian hearts:

> *Fairest Lord Jesus! Ruler of all nature!*
> *O Thou of God and man the Son!*
> *Thee will I cherish, Thee will I honor,*
> *Thou my soul's glory, joy, and crown.*

In 1680 amidst religious and political turmoil often brought on by the kings themselves, Joachim Neander was associated with Calvin Reformed church in Germany. He wrote this hymn set to a tune composed by Erneurten Gesangbuch of Stralsund:

> *Praise to the Lord, the Almighty, the King of creation!*
> *O my soul, praise Him, for He is thy health and salvation!*
> *All ye who hear, now to His temple draw near;*
> *Join me in glad adoration!*

RUMANIAN TRANSLATION OF THE BIBLE: In 1688, a group of scholars translated the Bible from the Septuagint into the language of their people.

This same year came the death of one of the most well-known restorationists, John Bunyan. For preaching in England without being ordained, he was imprisoned.

During that time he wrote the most famous Christian book outside the Bible in history: *Pilgrim's Progress.* He held membership in the church of Christ, but later the Baptists claimed him.

In 1693 in England, Thomas Shepherd wrote this hymn to spread courage and a reason for it all among the persecuted:

> *Must Jesus bear the cross alone,*

And all the world go free?
No, there's a cross for everyone,
And there's a cross for me.

The consecrated cross I'll bear
Till he shall set me free,
And then go home my crown to wear,
For there's a crown for me.

In 1704, Benjamin Schmolke wrote this hymn of courage and hope:

My Jesus, as Thou wilt!
All shall be well with me;
Each changing future scene
I gladly trust with Thee;

Straight to my home above
I travel calmly on,
And sing, in life or death,
"My Lord, Thy will be done."

But this century brought the beginning of secularization into much of Europe. People were satisfied to be members of whatever church they were "born into." Many denominations took on infant baptism so that the child would grow up believing s/he was of that sect; a speculation that usually became true.

Possibly trying to urge Christians to penetrate the new philosophy, Laurentius Laurenti wrote this hymn:

Rejoice, all ye believers,
And let your lights appear;
The evening is advancing,
And darker night is near.

The Bridegroom is arising,
And soon He draweth nigh;
Up, pray, and watch, and wrestle;
At midnight comes the cry.

Further, religion moved from interest in the Scriptures to rationalizing one's sins, self-pietism, that parts of the Bible were mythical, a belief in science over faith. Europe began to lose interest in religion and replace it with the Renaissance arts.

During this ho-hum period of religion, worshippers in England did not have hymn books, so had to follow a leader who sang a verse, followed by the congregation who repeated the verse. Not many hymns were made available to the people at that time.

Isaac Watts decided to help the problem, and in 1707 published his *Hymns and Spiritual Songs,* the first hymn book in the English language. One of the hymns was:

> *I'm not ashamed to own my Lord,*
> *Nor to defend His cause;*
> *Maintain the honors of His Word,*
> *The glory of His cross.*

Another, among the 600 hymns he eventually wrote, was:

> *O God, our help in ages past,*
> *Our hope for years to come,*
> *Our shelter from the stormy blast*
> *And our eternal home.*

In 1709, Thomas Ken of England, amidst the continual shift of kings and religious alliances that he tried to keep happy, often in vain, wrote this hymn:

> *Praise God, from whom all blessings flow;*
> *Praise Him, all creatures here below;*
> *Praise Him above, ye heavenly host;*
> *Praise Father, Son and Holy Ghost.*

Three years later in 1712, Joseph Addison wrote this comforting hymn:

> *When all Thy mercies, O my God, my tender soul surveys.*
> *Transported with the view, I'm lost in wonder, love and praise.*

He also wrote these words set to the unforgettable music of Franz Joseph Hayden:

> *The spacious firmament on high,*

> With all the blue ethereal sky,
> And spangled heavens, a shining frame,
> Their great Original proclaim.
>
> The unwearied sun, from day to day
> Does his Creator's power display,
> And publishes to every land
> The work of an Almighty hand.

To the northeast, Erdmann Neumeister wrote this hymn in 1718:

> Sinners Jesus will receive:
> Sound this word of grace to all
> Who the heavenly pathway leave,
> All who linger, all who fall.
>
> Sing it o'er and o'er again:
> Christ receiveth sinful men;
> Make the message clear and plain:
> Christ receiveth sinful men.

In 1719, Isaac Watts wrote this Christmas (though Christmas wasn't being celebrated much then) hymn of triumph:

> Joy to the World! The Lord is come!
> Let earth receive her king.
> Let every heart prepare him room,
> And heaven and nature sing.

The fight to follow just the Bible without man's additions, continued. While reflecting all that was done to make freedom of religion and personal access to the Bible possible, Isaac Watts wrote this anthem:

> Am I a soldier of the cross, follower of the Lamb,
> And shall I fear to own His cause, or blush to speak His Name?
> Must I be carried to the skies on flowery beds of ease,
> While others fought to win the prize and sailed thru bloody seas?
>
> Are there no foes for me to face? Must I not stem the flood?
> Is this vile world a friend to grace to help me on to God?

Worship Changes Since the First Century

Since I might fight if I would reign, increase my courage, Lord;
I'll bear the toil, endure the pain, supported by Thy Word.

And back in England there arose two brothers, Charles and John Wesley, both unordained evangelists. At Oxford in 1728, Charles organized the Holy Club. Later in his life he would write some 6500 hymns, mostly paraphrases of the Bible.

When brother John arrived, he organized the Bible Moths Club and Super-Erogation Men, referring to their methodical ways of studying the Bible.

In 1735 John Wesley met the Moravians and were impressed with their calm faith and pietism. At a devotional gathering that year, while someone was reading Luther's commentary on Romans, "I felt my heart strangely warmed. I felt that I did trust in Christ, Christ alone, for salvation; and an assurance was given me that he had taken away my sins, even mine, and saved me from the law of sin and death."

Because of this "experience", he decided there should be no ritual attached to salvation. The established churches refused to let him preach there, so he began preaching to the poor in open fields. His revival swept through England. Although his original methodist clubs grew into nonconformist churches, after his death his followers named the new movement the Methodist church.

In 1738, Charles Wesley wrote this poem, later set to music by Thomas Campbell, a Scotsman who moved to America and began yet another movement among several that had already begun in that country to restore the simplicity of first-century worship:

And can it be that I should gain
An interest in the Savior's blood?
Died He for me, who caused His pain?
For me, who Him to death pursued?
Amazing love! How can it be
That Thou, my God, shouldst die for me?

The following year, he wrote this now-famous hymn:

Hark! The herald angels sing,

> *"Glory to the newborn King;*
> *Peace on earth and mercy mild,*
> *God and sinners reconciled!"*
>
> *Joyful, all ye nations rise;*
> *Join the triumph of the skies;*
> *With the angelic hosts proclaim,*
> *"Christ is born in Bethlehem!"*

Among his hundreds of other hymns was also this one, written in 1749:

> Soldiers of Christ, arise and put your armor on;
> Strong in the strength which God supplies,
> Through his beloved Son.

William Williams in Wales broke away from the "Established church." He preached everywhere in his home country away from established church buildings, despite blistering sun, drenching rain, and hunger. Among his 800 hymns was this one written in 1745:

> *Guide me, O Thou great Jehovah,*
> *Pilgrim through this barren land;*
> *I am weak, but Thou art mighty;*
> *Hold me with Thy powerful hand;*
> *Bread of heaven, feed me till I want no more.*

In 1748, the Roman church decided that no one receives grace and favors from God unless granted by the Virgin Mary.

ORDAINED MARY GRANTS ALL FAVORS

That same year in England, John Newton, captain of a slave ship, walked onto land and never returned to sea. Although he retained his captain's outfit, he became a minister. One of his 284 hymns was this one written soon after his conversion:

> *Amazing grace! How sweet the sound*
> *That saved a wretch like me!*

Worship Changes Since the First Century

> *I once was lost, but now am found,*
> Was blind, but now I see.

Also in England in 1755, Philip Doddridge, wrote 375 hymns, among them:

> *Awake, my soul, stretch every nerve,*
> *And press with vigor on;*
> *A heavenly race demands thy zeal,*
> *And an immortal crown.*

In the meantime, Robert Robinson, who had never been religious, changed his life at age 20 and was baptized into Christ. Eventually he began preaching in a small congregation in Cambridge. Among the hymns he wrote was this one, written in 1757, three years after his conversion:

> *Oh, Thou Fount of every blessing,*
> *Tune my heart to sing Thy grace;*
> *Streams of mercy, never ceasing,*
> *Call for songs of loudest praise.*

But during this same period of time, Germans, with great respect for Immanuel Kant, moved to a humanistic type of "Christianity" that resembled agnosticism - that God cannot be proven or disproven.

In 1765, Joseph Grigg, a Presbyterian in England, wrote these two hymns:

> Jesus, and shall it ever be,
> A mortal man ashamed of Thee?
> Ashamed of Thee, whom angels praise,
> Whose glories shine through endless days?

and

> *Behold a Stranger at the door!*
> *He gently knocks, has knocked before,*
> *Has waited long, is waiting still;*
> *You treat no other friend so ill.*

In 1769, tired of all the kings of Europe fighting over which would be their official religious affiliation, offenses of which were punishable by death, Italian Felice de Giardini wrote this famous hymn:

> *Come, Thou Almighty King, help us Thy name to sing;*
> *Help us to praise.*
> *Father all glorious, o'er all victorious,*
> *Come and reign over us, Ancient of Days.*

In 1775, Edward Perronet, a Huguenot of England, wrote this hymn:

> *All hail the power of Jesus' name!*
> *Let angels prostrate fall;*
> *Bring forth the royal diadem,*
> *And crown Him Lord of all!*

In 1782, John Fawcett of England wrote this hymn:

> *Rock of Ages, cleft for me,*
> *Let me hide myself in Thee;*
> *Let the water and the blood,*
> *From Thy riven side which flowed,*
> *Be of sin the double cure,*
> *Cleanse me from its guilt and power.*

And in France, under the influence of Voltaire, there was a complete denial in the existence of God, preferring personal morals over the immoral church they had lived with for so many centuries.

In 1787, George Keith wrote this hymn, seemingly trying to get through to those who were forsaking religion completely:

> How firm a foundation, ye saints of the Lord,
> Is laid for your faith in His excellent word!
> What more can He say than to you He hath said,
> ~ You who unto Jesus for refuge have fled?

That same year, Samuel Stennett of England wrote:

Worship Changes Since the First Century

Majestic sweetness sits enthroned upon the Saviour's brow;
His head with radiant glories crowned,
His lips with grace o'erflow.

The last of the imprisonments, tortures and barbarous executions of people who just wanted to follow the Bible outside the mainline Roman church was in France. It continued well into the next century.

FRANCE, the first of Europe to receive the gospel, either by the Apostle Simon (the Zealot) or Ireneaus who preached and lived most of his life in Lyons....

FRANCE, the stronghold of Christianity during the dark ages....

FRANCE the originator of the reformation movement and restoration movement four centuries before it became famous in Germany....

FRANCE, the Christian nation that now was **HEADED INTO ATHEISM.**

The strongest centers of the Restoration movement, by now, had moved to and was thriving in North America. How many centuries will it be before it, too, succumbs?

What will this New Age Movement ultimately bring to the new continent? The same? Agnosticism? ATHEISM?

And among the few God-believers left, how strong will Christianity be? Strong enough to stand up against New Agers who believe everyone's god is the true God and take us all the way back to the paganism of Jesus' time?

After all, we've been putting opinion and big organization above scripture all these centuries. Why stop now?

Interestingly, the center of Christianity in the first century was Jerusalem and the Middle East. It is almost non-existent there today. Then the stronghold moved to Turkey and southern Europe, but it is almost non-existent there now too. Then it moved to France, England, and Germany but it is almost non-

existent there now. Finally, it moved to North America. Will the same thing happen there? Then where to? The Orient, South America, Africa? The church always seems to have thrived only where it was being persecuted.

They said it wouldn't happen here.
They said it couldn't.

ENDNOTES

[1]. Forbush, William B., *Fox's Book of Martyrs*, Zondervan Publishing House, Grand Rapids, 1968, pg. 168ff

[2]. Fox, pg. 105

[3]. *The Holy Bible,* The World Publishing Co., Cleveland, "The Epistle Dedicatory" pg. 3-4

4]. Fox, pg. 111

[5]. Fox, pg. 114

BIBLIOGRAPHY

D'Aubigne, J. H. Merle, *History of the Reformation of the Sixteenth Century*, The Religious Tract Society, London, 1846

The Ecclesiastical History of Eusebius Pamphilus, Baker Book House, Grand Rapids, 1971

Encyclopedia Britannica, William Benton Publisher, Chicago, 1966

Forbush, William B., Editor, *Fox's Book of Martyrs,* Zondervan Publishing House, Grand Rapids, 1926

Goold, G. P., Editor, *Bede Historical Works: Ecclesiastical History of the English Nation,* Vol. I and II

Keyes, Nelson B., *Story of the Bible World,* Reader's Digest Assn, Pleasantville, NY, 1962

Lightfoot, J.B., Editor, *The Apostolic Fathers,* Baker Book House, Grand Rapids, 1965

McDonald, William J., Editor, *The New Catholic Encyclopedia,* McGraw-Hill, Chicago, 1962

North, James B., *From Pentecost to the Present,* College Press Publishing, Joplin, Mo., 1983

Simon, Edith, *Great Ages of Man: The Reformation,* Time-Life Books, NY, 1968

Burrage, Henry S., *[Ana]Baptist Hymn Writers and their Hymns,* Brown Thurston & Co., Portland, Maine, 1889

Wells, H. G., *The Outline of History,* Garden

4. NEW TESTAMENT-PATTERNED CHURCH

Europe 2nd — 15th Centuries

EXPLANATION OF DOCUMENTARY SOURCES

The New Testament church has always existed. What God began on the Day of Pentecost nearly 2000 years ago, he would never allow to die. God is not weak.

Because the only world headquarters of the New Testament church is heaven, there is no way to record just when and where all those New Testament-patterned congregations have existed down through the ages. We can only know by reading the writings each group handed down, or hearing them speak, both of which is usually not possible. Only with God is this possible.

Further, because the only world headquarters of the New Testament church is to be heaven, and the only other headquarters is to be the confines of the elders/presbyters of each congregation (I Timothy and Titus), records were only kept within a congregation.

There are basically three primary original documentary sources of information on various early congregations. (1) The major primary original source is documents filed and archived by their enemies. Until around the 19th century, governments selected an official religion, and their police could go around on Sunday mornings searching for houses or other meeting places of people not at the formal church. The offenders would be arrested and either fined, or tortured for a confession, and possibly then executed. Of course, all these proceedings were written in public records and archived, most of which are available to us today. (2) The second primary original documentary source is pamphlets and books written by the protesters who led people out of the government-selected religion to the simple New Testament church as set out by Jesus' apostles. These writings were more likely to be published after the invention of movable type. (3) The third primary original source is congregational minutes and letters, though not as plentiful as we would like.

Since most people do not have the time, or mental and physical energy to do such massive original documentary searches themselves, we rely on secondary sources wherein books are written by authors who have themselves done the research, and their books cite original documents, dates, and where they are archived. One of these secondary sources used at length in this book is *Fox's Book of Martyrs* by John Fox (1517-1587), approximately 370 pages.

A second such source is *One Thousand Years of churches of Christ in England: Traces of the Kingdom* with 658 pages by Keith Sisman, **https://www.chulavistabooks.com/products/10141-traces-of-the-kingdom/**

A third such source is *Tradition and History of the Early Churches of Christ In Central Europe*, by Dr. Hans Grimm and Translated by Dr. H. L. Schug, World Evangelism Publications, choate@WorldEvangelism.org, PO Box 72, Winona, MS 38967, USA. It is also on the internet at **http://www.netbiblestudy.net/history** This website includes a bibliography of primary sources in various languages that he consulted in writing his book. Dr. Grimm descended from one of the oldest New Testament Christian families in Germany, dating back to before 1100.

A final primary documentary source that only indirectly witnesses to congregations of the first-century-patterned church is translations of the Bible into a local language. With this, anyone could then have access to the simple pattern of the New Testament church, eliminate all the fancy things added by "human wisdom" that they may have inherited, and easily develop a New Testament-patterned congregation. As more translations were made, there grew up more protests.

What does it take to be part of the New Testament church of Christ as founded on the Day of Pentecost? Some claim there has to be a written list of unbroken successions through the centuries at one location. But that is like cutting a string a specified length, then cutting a second piece after that pattern, then a third one after the pattern of the second, and so on. Anyone with experience doing this knows those pieces of string cut later will probably not be true to the size of the one cut first.

Down through the ages, a New Testament-patterned congregation may have existed only 20 years, but during that time, started other congregations. Then, if it went out of existence, or changed its doctrine, the congregations they began still existed, therefore creating time overlaps.

We must keep in mind that the specific doctrinal drifting we have today did not always exist. For example, predestination was not ever considered until the mid-1500s. Instrumental music was never a real issue among all denominations until the late 1800s and early 1900s. But how we are saved, and how to organize and worship as stated in the Bible are always reliable measures.

And so it is that we trace the New Testament church through the ages. Most will not be represented here simply because our headquarters is in heaven. But, for now, read and be amazed.

2nd Century

Were these people you will read about below New Testament Christians? Up to now, the only <u>doctrinal</u> change in the church was development of a hierarchy with certain elders being put in charge of several congregations in a city, then another elder calling himself a bishop and being in charge of them. Infant baptism was introduced and pushed by some church leaders as a way of getting control of families while very young. Very few people believed in these things yet.

During the mid-to-late first century, Jesus' Apostle, Simon the Zealot, according to *Eusebius' Ecclesiastical History* and *Fox's Book of Martyrs*, established the New Testament church in Britain. Apparently he established congregations on his way there in both Spain and France. And it is likely he went over to the nearest border of Germany not too far away, and established the New Testament church there also. [1] Many of his congregations would still exist in the second century since persecution of Christians in these places had not begun yet.

According to *Reader's Digest Story of the Bible World,* by 185 AD, there were European congregations in Cologne and Mainz, GERMANY; Lyon in FRANCE; Leon, Saragossa and Merida in SPAIN, Carthage in northern AFRICA, and of course ITALY, GREECE and TURKEY as mentioned in the Bible.

(The following will not cover Christianity in Africa, the Middle-East, or the Orient, language barriers precluding a study of that history. It also will not cover today's Turkey and parts of Italy and Greece where apostles of the New Testament established congregations.) [2]

Apparently, the congregations in Europe were established by the students of the apostles called the "Apostolic Fathers." For example, Ireneaus was a life-time missionary to Lyons, Gaul (France). He was a student of Polycarp who had been a student of the Apostle John.

In Ireneaus' writings we find: "...we walk on the highways and sail withersoever we will without fear" (iv.30.1-31.I). [3]

BRITAIN

In 141 AD, in the area of today's Cambridgeshire and village of Grantchester near today's Cambridge "many were baptized." [4] Apparently this was a blooming of the seed of the word planted by apostle Simon the Zealot in the mid- to late-first century as noted above.

FRANCE

The stronghold of Christianity in the second century was France.

Ireneas was raised in a Christian family in today's Turkey, then went to Lyons, France, around 140 AD. He was careful to stay as close to the Scriptures as possible. Although he took an unscriptural title of bishop over a large area instead of just one congregation as directed in the Scriptures, there does not seem to be any other unscriptural practice in his life. He warned "therefore such as introduce other doctrines, hide from us the opinion which they themselves have concerning God; knowing the unsoundness and futility of their own doctrine, and fearing to be overcome, and so to have their salvation endangered" (iv.32.I) [5]

Other evidence we have of the New Testament church in France is found in *Eusebius,* Book V, Chapter 1, where he devoted fifteen pages to telling about the persecutions they endured. Amphitheaters were built for the purpose of watching slow execution of Christians by various means both in Lyons and Vienna.

Their crime was so-called cannibalism because they ate the body and blood of Jesus (at the Lord's Supper) every Sunday, and incest because they married their (spiritual) brothers and sisters. They ranged in age from 15 to 90, both men and women. One was a physician.

After their arrest, they were dragged to prison with the crowds beating up on them or throwing stones at them as they passed. Tortures continued in prison day after day. They were put on the rack to get them to recant being Christians. One man had red hot plates of brass placed on the most tender parts of his body. After he died, his body was "one continued wound, mangled and shriveled, that had entirely lost the form of man to the external eye."

If the foregoing did not kill them, Romans citizens were beheaded. The rest were taken to the amphitheater where they were sent through a gauntlet of scourges and dragged around by wild beasts. If this did not kill them, they were then placed in a hot chair to be roasted to death. One woman endured it all, still without being killed. Thereupon she was put in a net and cast before a bull who killed her. [6]

Keep in mind that most of the variations in doctrine we have today did not exist then. In fact, various Catholic and protestant groups with opposing doctrines claim Irenaeus as their own, groups that did not even exist in his time.

GERMANY

According to George Trabert in his *Church History* of 1897, there were independent congregations of the Lord's church in today's Germany at Strasburg, Trier, Augsburg, and along the Rhine River.

Since the Roman Empire version of overly-organized and overly-formalized Christianity was not popularized until the mid-300s, every congregation in remote areas was on its own based on the Scriptures that would have been taken to them by the missionaries.

3rd Century

Baptism by sprinkling was introduced, but only for the very sick. Elders began claiming they were the only ones who could impart the Holy Spirit on baptized believers. Much more serious was another power play wherein a priest elevated the bread and wine of the Lord's Supper and told people to worship it because it became the actual body and blood of Jesus. This was called transubstantiation. This was also a way to get people to stop keeping the Lord's Supper among themselves without church hierarchy. None of these things were widely accepted, but the "church" leaders kept pushing it. It would give them more power over the common Christian.

Both *Eusebius' Ecclesiastical History* and *Fox's Book of Martyrs* written in the mid-1500s, tell of persecution of Christians in western Europe because they had established the New Testament church there among the pagans. Unless otherwise indicated in this report, references to all countries but Britain are often taken from *Fox's Book of Martyrs*.

BRITAIN

There was severe persecution of Christians all over the Roman Empire, including Britain, during the reigns of Decius (c.AD 254) and Septimus Severus (c.AD 209). It was during this time that an itinerate underground preacher (identified centuries later by the Catholic church as one of their priests) converted a British-Roman officer named Alban in Hertfordshire.

As explained in David Nash Ford's *Early British Kingdoms*, this itinerate preacher has been identified as Amphibalus. At a time when he was being sheltered and supported by Alban, Roman soldiers entered his home in search of Amphibalus. Alban exchanged cloaks with the preacher, so it was Alban who was executed. Alban was first scourged for refusing to sacrifice to idols, and then ordered beheaded. His would-be executioner was so impressed with this Jesus that Alban was willing to die for, he requested to be executed in his place. On June 22, 287 they were both beheaded.

Apparently the itinerate preacher escaped to Wales where he continued to preach. In the following century, Constantine legalized Christianity throughout the Roman Empire. Please note, that even though various religious groups have declared both Alban and Amphibalus as saints, it is certain they did not go by such a title since the Bible says all Christians are saints. In fact, declaring someone a saint did not even begin until the tenth century, and that only in the Catholic church.

Emperor Constantine the Great died in 337 AD. We do not have a birth date, but considering his rise to power the first of the fourth century, he obviously was born in the third century, possibly around 265. His mother was Helena, married to Roman Senator Constantius, a legate in Britain.

G. K. Chesterton in his book, *A Short History of England*, stated that she was considered a Briton by the British. Some people believe she came from Colchester in Essex; today the town has schools and places named after her, as well as her image appearing on the town hall.

Constantine's maternal grandfather was king of Coel in Colchester. This is based in part on ancient British Sozoman's *Historia Ecclesiastica* , written in the 400s Remember, there was no thought of modern diversions from the New Testament doctrine such as instrumental music, predestination, etc. Christianity was still simple. His mother apparently did not believe in infant baptism, because Constantine was not baptized until the next century. Baptism remained by immersion until the twelve century.

FRANCE

In Nice, France, Trypho and Respicius were imprisoned for believing Jesus was the Son of God. Nails were pounded through their feet, then they were forced to run or be dragged through the street. Back in prison they were scourged, torn with large iron hooks, scorched with lighted torches, and finally beheaded on February 1, 251.

In 257 in Toulouse, France, the Christian Saturninus was arrested for refusing to sacrifice to an idol. After being tortured and returned to the idol temple, his feet were fastened to the tail of a bull. The enraged animal was then driven down the temple steps until our brother's head burst open.

In 287 in Acquitain, France, a Christian woman named Faith was broiled on a gridiron and then beheaded.

Also that year, two Christians named Quintin and Lucian went to Amiens, France, and then to Beaumaris. Lucian was martyred. Quinton went on to Picardy. There he was put on the rack and stretched with pullies until his joints were dislocated. He was also torn with wire scourges, endured boiling oil and pitch poured over him as well as lighted torches burning him. He died in prison shortly after.

SPAIN

In 259 in Tarragon, Spain, Fructuosus, Augurius and Eulogius were burned at the stake for believing Jesus was the Son of the only God, being New Testament Christians.

4th Century

This was the century that Constantine made Christianity legal, set up a church hierarchy in the pattern of ancient Roman government, and called it the Holy Roman Empire. The first creed was put into effect which they called the "Apostles' Creed" though the apostles had been dead for over three centuries. Celibacy of church leaders was introduced, but not widely accepted yet.

BRITAIN

At Richborough is a castle built by the Romans when they landed in Britain in AD 43. This castle has an adult-size baptismal font for immersions on its grounds. The font was built in the fourth century. This, then, indicates that the church continued to exist in Britain and people were being baptized by immersion to become Christians.

RUSSIA TO FRANCE AND SPAIN

In 308, God was about to use a barbarian warrior to further strengthen the New Testament church in France and Spain. According to Origen around 200 AD, the New Testament church had been established in Russia (then called Scythia) by the Apostle Andrew late in the first century.

The areas of northern Greece and northeast to Russia around the Black Sea were occupied by the Goths. In Pannonia (later known as Hungary), Christian Quirinus was arrested, chained heavily and put on display from town to town along the Danube River. In the city of Sabaria, a stone was fastened about his neck and he was drowned.

Although the Christians probably had writings left behind by Andrew, it was good for them to have the entire New Testament. In the mid-300s, an alphabet was created for the Goths. The Bible was then translated into that language from the original Greek. This is all they needed to know to make sure they were organizing and worshipping according to the New Testament first century pattern.

Then Attila the Hun arrived with his army. The Goths during the next hundred years gradually moved across southern Europe. They ended up in southern France (Gaul) and Spain. They had taken their Bible translated in their own language with them. The Goths remained in control of Spain and France for the next 350 years.

Therefore, the Christianity of western Europe would have been fairly untainted, but also fairly strong before the Roman Empire was able to effectively spread its religious wings to that area.

These Goths were never Roman Catholics or Jews, although they treated both minority groups with respect. They were Christians who rejected worship of the Lord's Supper as the actual presence of Jesus. They had the Bible available to everyone written in their own language. These Scriptures were never suppressed until the Roman Catholics grew powerful enough to do so.

FRANCE

In 303 in Marseilles, France, the Christian named Victor spent his fortune on relieving the poor in his congregation, and visiting them at night to comfort them. Arrested by a pagan government, he was dragged through the street while the crowd further degraded him in other ways. In prison he was placed on the rack, and finally returned to a dungeon.

While there he converted his jailers, Alexander, Felician and Longinus. The governor ordered that he be put back on the rack, beaten with batoons, and returned to the dungeon. On a third occasion he was ordered by the pagan governor to offer incense to a small idol. He kicked the idol and altar over, and that foot was immediately cut off. He was then thrown into a mill where he was crushed with the stones.

SPAIN

In 304 in Terragona where the New Testament church existed, Valerius an elder, and Vincent a deacon, were arrested for their faith, chained with heavy irons, and dragged to prison. Valerius was banished.

Vincent was placed on the rack until his joints were dislocated. His flesh was torn with large hooks. Then he was placed on a gridiron with fire under him and spikes over him that were driven into him. Still not recanting his belief in Jesus, he was put in a dark dungeon with sharp flints and broken glass on the floor where he died.

5th Century

The unscriptural development of a church hierarchy made another step toward getting control of the Christian world. They introduced ministers wearing clothes that were different from everyone else, calling them priests. They also began an effort to get control of the Scriptures and not allow anyone to read them. Neither was widely accepted, but it was growing in places like Italy and Egypt.

BRITAIN

Infant baptism was reintroduced 407, but hardly anyone agreed with it or conformed to it. It was still another ploy to get control of people's lives by a growing and unscriptural church hierarchy. However, their Bishop Germanus filed a complaint that the British church was practicing only believer baptism. Actually, infant baptism still was not widely accepted.

FRANCE

John Cassian lived in the late fourth and early fifth centuries, and wrote of spiritual matters. He lived and wrote in Marseille in southern France. He was condemned by Catholic church leaders around 428 because he opposed the teachings of Augustine about Rome being the city of God, etc., and had many followers throughout southern France. John has been called a monk by many historians, a term loosely applied to many who were merely ministers of the gospel.

SCOTLAND & IRELAND

Early in this century the church spread to Scotland and Ireland, probably as a result of missionary work done by the students of the Apostle Simon (the Zealot) in Britain.

In 430, Ninian, who had been educated in Rome, tried to set up congregations, of course with Roman church beliefs, but met with resistance. Both the Scottish and Irish churches were distinct from the Roman church in many things. Later Rome coerced them to live a Catholic or face severe persecutions, tortures and death.

Late in this century when Patrick did missionary work in Ireland and tried to set up diocese with bishops over them, he met with resistance. These people obviously knew from the New Testament that elders/presbyters/bishops were to be heads of only one congregation.

6th Century

Strong efforts were made to have a bishop in Rome made head of the church worldwide. When most Christians heard about it, they rebelled against it. It took centuries of papal wars to finally pull people into line.

BRITAIN, IRELAND, SCOTLAND

In the late 500s a group of Christians began being called Paulicians because they defended their beliefs with the New Testament, especially the writings of the Apostle Paul. They called each other brother and sister, and taught that faith and repentance were requirements of baptism, and it was by immersion.

As the rest of Europe headed into the Dark Ages, in the Celtic northern European territory, especially Britain and Ireland, education and reading flourished. Beautiful books such as the Lindisfarne Gospels survive from this period. With education flourishing, people could read the Bible for themselves and worship just as Christians in the first century did.

BULGARIA AND FRANCE

The Christians who were nicknamed Paulicians by their enemy for insisting on reading the Bible for themselves, were heavily persecuted by the Catholic church, so eventually fled to Bulgaria and nearby countries.

7th Century

The church in Rome declared that their ordinances were as sacred as the Bible, another ploy to build up personal interests and riches by getting control of the Christians. Of course, it was unscriptural. Also they declared that only certain things could be said at the Lord's Supper, another step toward taking away the ability of people to keep the Lord's Supper in their house churches.

BRITAIN

The New Testament church in Britain had been personally started by the Apostle Simon the Zealot. During this century the Roman church sent missionaries to Britain. These representatives from Rome tried to convert them to fall in line with Roman teachings. But the British Christians overall remained true to the teachings of their apostle. They rejected celibacy of the clergy, confession to priests, infant baptism, and so on.

Augustine followers led a massacre at Bangor, Wales, where some 1200 members of the church were slaughtered. These Christians belonged to independent congregations and taught adult believer baptism. The Catholic church called their leaders monks, but they had their own homes, were married, and had a secular job, and so were just independent preachers of the gospel, not monks.

Church buildings still did not exist. But in 627, King Edwin built his own baptistery.

GERMANY

A Christian named Killien was raised a Christian and went to preach in Franconia, Germany. In Wurtzburg he converted Gozbert, the governor. Later, an opponent in the royal house had him beheaded in 689.

8th Century

This century, the church at Rome declared its bishop/pope was head of the church worldwide. It also ordained images be made of Jesus, Mary and the apostles, and all Christians were now required to bow to those images.

BRITAIN

In Britain, the Bible was first given to the people in what we today call Old English, a combination of German, French and Latin, by Caedman. Although it was in the form of poetry and not an actual translation, it gave the common people an opportunity to read for themselves. Also about this time, Bede made an actual translation of parts of the Bible.

Therefore, all the people had to do who wanted to worship the way people did in the first century, was to read their Bibles. Later the Roman church was able to influence government officials here. But they had trouble getting the Brits themselves to fall in line with them.

When the pope quoted Matthew 16:19 saying the keys of the kingdom were given to Peter only, they wrote the pope back quoting Matthew 18:18 saying the keys of the kingdom had been given to all the apostles.

9th Century

The hierarchy at Rome commanded that bishops had to place the bread of the Lord's Supper on the tongues of worshipers. Although it had been optional in the past, all church officers (priests, bishops, etc.) were now required to wear "holy" vestments and dress different from the average Christian.

GERMANY

The Bible was translated into the German language by an unknown translator. We must always conclude that, whenever and where ever the Bible was translated into the language of a people, they learned for themselves what God wanted of them, and there were always those who insisted on following the Apostle Peter's advice: "We ought to obey God rather than man". After all, God said, "My Word will not return to Me void." Believing that, we must believe that whenever and wherever the Bible was made available to people, churches of Christ rose up.

THE SLAVS

In Moravia, the Slavic alphabet was invented. Then the Bible was translated into the language of the people. It was called the *Old Church Slavonic Bible*. So, although their King Boris in Bulgaria nearby, affiliated with the central church in Constantinople, they still had the Bible and could still meet the way Christians in the first century did.

Anyone wanting to organize and worship the same way people did in the first century could then just read the Bible for themselves and do so.

10th Century

Although religious writers often refer to certain early church leaders as saints, it wasn't until this century that the church hierarchy in Rome declared that it should be done. It was never on the minds of early church leaders! After all, the Scriptures state that all Christians are saints.

BRITAIN

Old English was in the process of changing into what we today call Middle English. In Britain, in 995, Aelfric wrote so many articles about Scriptures in the Old and New Testaments that he ended up quoting most of it. Thus, people could still refer to the writings of the Bible in their own language to organize and worship the same way Christians did in the first century.

EUROPE

The *Encyclopedia Britannica,* discussing the Waldenses, states that there were numerous "sects" (anyone who was not Roman Catholic) during the Middle Ages, but they are obscure because they did not have writings of their own defending their faith; rather they chose to remain to themselves, being congregational in organization.

All we know of them is what their enemies wrote about them. But later they would find it necessary to write letters and tracts defending their New Testament views. "In early times these sectaries produced little literature of their own." They had no need to. The New Testament was all the literature they needed.

"When they produced a literature at the beginning of the 15th century, they attempted to claim for it a much earlier origin....the historical continuity of Protestantism from the earliest times.

"According to this view the church was pure and uncorrupt till the time of Constantine (350 AD) when Sylvester gained the first temporal possession for the papacy, and so began the system of a rich, powerful and worldly church, with Rome for its capital.

"Against this secularized church a body of witnesses silently protested; they were always persecuted but always survived." [6]

11th Century

The church at Rome declared that no priest could be married. Those who were married were forced to give up their wives and children. If they did not, the wives and children were made permanent slaves of the church. Worse, they now officially declared that the bread of the Lord's Supper definitely became the actual body of Jesus, and the wine became the actual blood of Jesus, so should be worshiped. This had been declared in the past, but now it was enforced. This belief is called transubstantiation. Objectors were easy to identify because they refused to bow down to the emblems. They were arrested and heavily persecuted.

BRITAIN

The French conquered Britain in 1066. The church of Christ had always been strong in France, and some of those who followed the conquerors into England brought their beliefs with them. The first major religious writing published in English was *Represser of Over-Much Weeting [Criticizing] of the Clergie,*' opposing the Lollards who called themselves Christians, the church, the church of Christ. They baptized believers by immersion.

FRANCE

Around 1010 in France, a man named Berengarius (Berengar of Tours) preached Gospel truths according to the primitive ways of the first century. He insisted that the Lord's Supper was a symbolic memorial service and not to be worshipped. He insisted that the Bible was the only foundation of faith, not church rules and traditions. People called his followers Berengarians. They just wanted to be called Christians. They spread throughout France, Germany, Italy and England.

About that same time, Peter Bruis (de Bruys), who had heard Berengarius, taught similarly with his followers completely separating from the church of Rome. He wrote a book against the pope entitled ANTICHRIST. Outsiders called this group Petrobusians, although they considered themselves simply Christians.

Some of their beliefs were as follows: (1) The Lord's Supper should be kept as a memorial, and not as a mass where it is worshipped; (2) Ministers should marry; (3) Infant baptism is never found in the Scriptures; (4) churches need not be officially consecrated; (5) Holding masses for the dead is not in the Bible and should not be practiced.

Peter was arrested by the advocates of the Catholic church and burned alive at St. Giles, about 50 miles from Marseille.

GERMANY & NETHERLANDS

Around mid-century, the Four Gospels were translated from Latin into the language of West Saxony which today is the western part of Germany and the Netherlands.

In 1025, according to research done by Hans Godwin Grimm and published in his *Tradition and History of the churches of Christ in Central Europe*, the Catholic Archbishop of Cambrai wrote of some repentant heretics of Lorraine who formerly claimed the original church of Christ did not believe in purgatory, transubstantiation, sin inherited by babies, sprinkling in place of immersion, instrumental music, bowing before images, creation of special saints, and veneration of Mary.

They had been taught by an Italian missionary named Gundulf who stated that there were independent congregation of "true Christians" in the Rhineland and Alsace, and in Switzerland. This information was apparently gleaned from a search of medieval government records in Germany. Dr. Grimm's ancestor was burned at the stake in 1118 for being a New Testament Christian and belonging to an independent congregation. He stated his grandfather had been converted and baptized by immersion for forgiveness of his sins by a missionary from Italy. It is estimated that his grandfather was born around 1028. (Read more about this below.)

Grimm further stated that there were many churches of Christ in central Germany, and in 1052 the most outspoken of their preachers were burned at the stake in Goslar. Again, he apparently obtained this information from medieval government archives.

12th Century

During this century, the practice of substituting pouring or sprinkling for immersion baptism began to spread widely.

BRITAIN

The Hillcliffe church of Christ was established around 1157 in Oxford, Cheshire, by thirty New Testament Christians. By 1166, another eighty Christian brothers and sisters had been added to the congregation. Many were examined before King Henry II and the English parliament. Their leaders preached the gospel to the king and parliamentarians. They believed in autonomous congregations, baptism of adults by immersion for forgiveness of sins, and patterned themselves after the true church of Christ, not a man-organized denomination. Eventually they built a small chapel with a cemetery dating from 1643 and still existing today.

Another congregation was established some two miles north of this congregation in Warrington, Lancashire. Whenever church authorities got close to finding them, or when they were found and persecution ensued, members of the two congregations would change locations with each other, and probably worshiped together sometimes too.

The Paulicians that rose up in the late sixth century in France and Germany eventually made their way to Britain where they were usually called Publicans or German Hereticks. A "monk" identified as Radulph complained that saints should not be prayed to, there is no purgatory, and infants should not be baptized.

Many fled to Europe. Three elders were Dulcinus, Nauarensis and Gerhardus. Nauarensis and his wife, Margaret, fled to Europe, but were killed by the Catholic church there. Others stayed in Britain and survived during the time of Wycliffe and other restoration leaders.

FRANCE

Around the turn of the century, a Mr. Grimm of Ensisheim, was baptized by immersion for forgiveness of his sins by a traveling merchant from Venetia, who in turn was from the "only church of the saints". In 1118, Mr. Grimm baptized his grandson, Gregory Grimm. The grandson was tortured by Catholic authorities.

By 1143, the government took into custody an entire congregation with these beliefs, and all were tortured. They confessed that such independent congregations were meeting secretly all over France. Since each congregation had its own elders and deacons and no centralized headquarters, the authorities were sometimes unsuccessful in finding them.

In Toulouse, France, in 1147 another congregation of the New Testament church began to be called by outsiders Henricians. Their leader was Henry of Toulouse. He was a former "monk" who believed as Peter De Bruys had. These Christians were centered in Tours. They declared that Christians could do nothing except that which came directly from Scriptures themselves. A letter written by Everinus wrote to Bernard (a future "saint" of the Catholic church) in 1146 complained that these Henricians rejected infant baptism and had formed a "church of Christ" separate from the Catholic church. The elders of this congregation were burned at the stake.

In 1147 Bernard accused the Earl of St. Giles of protecting Henry of Toulouse whom he identified as a heretic who taught believer baptism, elimination of clergy, and independence from the Catholic church.

Peter Waldo/Valdo, was a native of Lyons where the Apostolic Father, Irenaeus had established the New Testament church. Around 1170, he openly opposed the church at Rome. People began calling his followers Waldenses or Waldoys.

Alarmed at his effectiveness in spreading the New Testament church wherever he traveled, in 1179, Pope Alexander III ordered him to cease preaching except by direct consent of the local Roman bishop. This did not work, so in 1184 he ordered all Waldenses exterminated. The French tried to oblige him. It began in Toulouse and spread to Province, an area in extreme southern France. So they escaped to Italy.

ITALY

Peter Waldo, merchant from Lyons, France, preached widely in the valleys of Piedmont in northern Italy. His followers were identified by enemies as Waldensians. The inhumane torture they endured at the hands of the Catholic church are, in some instances, too hideous to print. Their sin? Following only the Scriptures.

In 1155 in northern Italy, Arnold of Brescia and the simple Christians with him declared that it was unscriptural for....

1. The church to own property.
2. Ministers and bishops to control the civil government.

He was hanged at the request of Pope Adrian IV. Still the New Testament church refused to die.

BULGARIA

Many Christians in the Balkans, especially Bulgaria, were discovered by church authorities, some having fled from France. So many such "heretics" were discovered there, tortured and burned, that the name "Bulgare" came to be synonymous with "Heretic" and eventually "Bugger".

NETHERLANDS AND BULGARIA

Godwin Grimm stated in his book, *Tradition and History of the churches of Christ in Central Europe,* that the church of Christ was strong in the Netherlands, and congregations there were in regular contact with other independent congregations in Greece, Macedonia, Bulgaria, and Alsace-Lorraine.

GERMANY

In Germany, the first reported Christian martyr by papal decree was the death of an apparent ancestor of Godwin Grimm, Gregorius Grimm around 1118.

"Standing before the tribunal he solemnly declared: 'If there is here a heretic, not I can be called heretic, for having been buried with Christ in the water of rebirth, I also have had by this baptism remission of my sins. I have been raised by Christ from spiritual death. I received Him and He gave me the power to enter the realm of God to become a happy child of my heavenly Father.'

"Interrogated on his teachings, he answered that already his grandfather had been baptized in the little river Fecht by an Italian missionary, and that he supposed that the majority of his fellow believers are inhabitants of Macedonia. But neither the breaking of his arms and legs by the torture nor the flames of the stake where he was burned alive in 1118 could make him tell the names of the little group of Alsatian Christians he belonged to."

Grimm stated that his ancestor's congregation at that location still exists: "From this remarkable year of 1118 we can trace the story of the little church in Alsatia to our days. In the records of the Roman Catholic inquisition they appear as "Ortlibarii," "Runcarii" or "Beghardi," whereas the people called them "Christ's poor disciples" ("Arme Junger Christi") or "Good People" ("Gutleute"). But they themselves never used another name for their congregations but "Christengemeine" ("church of Christ") and for the members of these churches as "Christen" ("Christians") or Brethren and Sisters in Christ."

13th Century

With more and more translations of the Bible being made into the language of the common people, the Catholic church hierarchy at Rome made it church law that no one could study the Scriptures without a church official being present. Thus, power-hungry religious leaders unabashedly took the Scriptures from the common Christian in order to destroy proof that their power was not allowed in the Scriptures.

BRITAIN

By 1235, there were many secret congregations of the church of Christ in Britain. They met in Rochester, Chilterns, Worcester and elsewhere. They endured through the time of Edward III, Richard I, King John, and Henry III. Around 1235, the Friars Minoritis arrived in England ready to force the "heretics" to denounce their beliefs in congregational autonomy, baptism by immersion for remission of sins, and calling themselves the church of Christ instead of the Catholic church. Everywhere, these brave New Testament Christians taught primarily from the scripture Mark 16:15 and 16.

ITALY

Here the Waldenses translated the Bible into the language of the Italian people.

Eventually there were two large groups of them involving many congregations scattered north of the Alps and down into northern Italy. Their beliefs were nearly identical.

North of the Alps: (1) Oaths are forbidden by the gospel; (2) Capital punishment is not allowed to the civil power; (3) All Christians are priests; therefore any layman may consecrate the sacrament of the Lord's Supper; (4) The Roman church is not the New Testament church; (5) Asceticism is not a requirement of Christianity.

Northern/Lombardy, Italy: (1) Oaths are forbidden by the gospel; (2) Capital punishment is not allowed to the civil power; (3) All Christians are priests; therefore any layman may consecrate the sacrament of the Lord's Supper as long as they were not in mortal sin; (4.) The Roman church is not the New Testament church, but is the scarlet woman of the Apocalypse, whose precepts ought not to be obeyed, especially those appointing fast-days; (5) Asceticism is not a requirement of Christianity.

Many fled to the Alps in valleys of Piedmont, and settled in valleys named after them, the Vaudois. Persecution continued in the lower regions.

GERMANY

Grimm explained in his book, "The Roman Catholic church and the German Emperor emulated in suppressing the original church of Christ; from 1118 to 1518, at least 4,000 Christians in Central Europe had to suffer a dreadful death for God's sake."

NETHERLANDS

During this century, several translations of the Bible into the common language of the people in the Netherlands came into being, names of translators unknown. But the author of the Bible was always known—God, not man.

14th Century

The Romans church hierarchy needed more money for palaces for its bishops and cathedrals, so told people they could buy their loved ones out of purgatory with indulgences.

BRITAIN

In the 1100s, independent congregations of the church of Christ were called Waldensians by their enemies. By the 1300s from Rochester to Chilterns to Worcester, they were called Lollards. But they called themselves the church of Christ. They were independent congregations who were baptized by immersion for forgiveness of their sins, and continued through the centuries to emphasize Mark 16:15-16.

By the 1330s, records of their enemies in the government-selected official religion, show these congregations were active in Wales, Bristol, Kent, Essex, Cambridgeshire, Lincolnshire, Newcastle, Yorkshire, and Furness Falls.

John Wycliffe was born in Yorkshire, England 1320. In 1382, Wycliffe completed his translation of the Latin Bible into English, the language of the common person, with the aid of Nicholas Hereford and John Purvey. He also sent out preachers throughout England. His preachers were to supplement the services of the church with religious instruction in the vernacular. The commoners, with their new knowledge, continued to denounce evils of the church, especially among the rich.

In 1379 he wrote public attacks on the pope. He also began formal attacks on the "new" Catholic doctrine of the Lord's Supper, transubstantiation, saying that in spirit only the bread and wine actually became Christ, but not materially.

Wycliffe was popular among churches of Christ, and those most closely associated with him were called by outsiders "mutterers," or "Lollards" probably because they continually murmured against the Roman church.

Later, a friend of Wycliffe, Nicholas of Hereford of Queen's College in England, became a spokesman for the independent congregations. Then Philip Repingdon carried the movement to Leichester where, by 1382, William Swinderby led a group of adherents into neighboring towns. In 1390-92, he was hidden by sympathizers in Wales

Dr. Hans Grimm wrote in his history of the early churches of Christ in Central Europe, "Even as late as 1390 A.D. a New Testament church in Celtic Hill Cliff in Wales built a room for worship with a great basin for immersion of adults in baptism on confession of faith."

John Purvey compiled the second translation of the Bible, more idiomatic and readable than Hereford's. He preached in Bristol. He declared these "Twelve Conclusions" in 1395 and presented them to the English Parliament:

(1) The present priesthood was not the one ordained by Christ; (1) The Roman ritual of ordination had no warrant in Scripture; (3) Clerical celibacy created unnatural lust; (4) Feigned miracle of transubstantiation led men into idolatry; (5) Hallowing wine, bread, altars, and vestments was related to necromancy (witchcraft); (6) Prelates should not be temporal judges and rulers; (7) Prayers for the dead must be condemned; (8) Pilgrimages must be condemned; (9) Offerings to images must be condemned; (10) Confession to a priest unnecessary to salvation; (11) Warfare is unscriptural; (12) Vows of chastity by nuns led to abortion and child murder; (13) Unnecessary flamboyant pursuit of the arts by the church encouraged waste; (14) The prime duty of priests is to preach; (15) All men should enjoy free access to the vernacular Scriptures.

FRANCE

The Anglo-Norman Translation of the Bible was done in part, but never completed. The Anglo-Normans were of Viking descent and lived mostly in the northern part of France.

BOHEMIA / CZECHOSLOVAKIA

Also in the middle of the fourteenth century, Jan (Johan) Milic of Kromeriz led a Bohemian national reform movement. He was a wealthy Christian who deliberately embraced poverty to preach return to the simplicity of the primitive New Testament church. He died in 1374.

His pupils founded the Bethlehem chapel in Prague where

public sermons were preached in Czech in the spirit of Milic's teachings. From 1402, Huss preached at the chapel.

GERMANY

In 1366, the Bible was translated literally word for word from the Latin into the common language of the people in Germany. It was this Bible that, a century later, would be the first one reproduced on a printing press.

Grimm reported that there were strongholds of New Testament Christianity in Poland, Ukraine, Austria, and Germany. Most of their preachers were arrested and executed, usually by torture.

15th Century

The rosary and choirs were introduced into the Catholic church. Also, Mary was elevated to mother of mankind.

BRITAIN

In the early 15th century, members of the church of Christ in Ludschurch, Staffordshire met secretly during times of severe persecution in a deep chasm 60 feet deep and 300 feet long in the Black Forest of White Peak.

William Sawtre (Sawtrey), another leader of this independent congregations movement was burned in 1401. In 1407, Oxford University fired all of its "Lollard" professors.

Keep in mind that this movement was spread, not so much by the peasants, but by leaders with some influence and who had money to help support fleeing Christians trying to avoid persecution.

Sir John Oldcastle, Knight, Lord of Cobham, was one of the most powerful men in Britain. In Olchen Valley, Wales, where he lived, he learned the New Testament pattern of becoming a

Christian and was baptized in a brook that runs through the valley in the Black Mountains. Small congregations were able to exist without much trouble. They even had their own secret building half cut into rock on the side of a mountain.

He paid for the training of many traveling preachers, apparently having what we might call today a preacher-training school on his estate in Kent. He was good friends with King Henry IV, who protected him. But when Henry died in 1413, his son, Henry V, became king and allowed the official state-selected church to arrest Sir Oldcastle for leading an uprising.

He escaped the Tower of London and fled to his home in Wales, now being considered a traitor. He was found and re-arrested in 1417, and taken back to London. That December he was led to public torture in fields near Lincoln's Inn, part of today's expanded London. He suddenly knelt and prayed for his enemies, and proclaimed to bystanders what the Scriptures said about salvation. Thereupon, the soldiers cut his stomach open, hung him between two poles by chains, then slowly roasted him to death. Throughout it all, rather than recant, he continued to proclaim to the bystanders what they must do to be saved.

Two years earlier in 1415, and thirty years after John Wycliffe's death, Wycliffe was declared a heretic on 267 counts by the government-selected church. His writings were burned, then his bones were burned and cast into the River Swift near the River Avon.

Between 1424 and 1430, hundreds were arrested in various cities in Norwich, Somerset and Lincoln.

In 1428, Abraham (NLN), Milburn White, and John Wade, at Colchester, rebelled against the Catholic church, desiring to be Christians only. They were arrested by the church for rebuffing transubstiation, a new doctrine declaring that the bread of the Lord's Supper became the actual body of Jesus Christ, and the wine became the actual blood of Jesus, and therefore should be bowed down to and worshiped. But that was not all. They also believed the true church was not the Catholic church, but any congregation of Christians who had been baptized into Christ by immersion. Further, they believed (1) No one should be required to keep holy days declared by the Catholic church such as Lent; (2) The pope was the antichrist; (3) Priests may marry; (4) Pilgrimages were not scriptural; (5) Images and relics should not be worshiped; (6) Christians should not pray to "saints"; (7) Only believer baptism of adults is acceptable.

White was burned at the stake near Bishopsgate, Norwich. Abraham was burned at the stake in Colchester. John Wadden was burned at the stake in Colchester. John Wade was burned at the stake in London. These we know by name from Catholic records; but many other New Testament Christians were arrested in Colchester and Norwich and burned at the stake.

In 1431, a former priest, Thomas Bagley of Malden, Essex, was caught preaching the gospel, arrested, and burned at the stake in Smithfield, London. In 1439, another former priest, Richard Wick, was burned at the stake on Tower Hill for preaching the simple New Testament gospel.

Another trick was now used, this time against wives of men who were teaching the gospel. They were accused of witchcraft. They were not allowed to defend themselves at their trials because one could not believe a witch. In tracing where the most numerous witch trials occurred, the church of Christ was most represented. These Christian wives were burned to death.

The Coleman Street church of Christ was formed in London in the 1400s and still existed in the 1500s. It was made up of both the working class and professional class. The latter were members of guilds and were primarily small manufacturers and merchants.

The Chestertown church of Christ in Cambridge believed the following, according to records of the Lord Bishop of Ely Gray: (1) Autonomous congregations, (2) baptism by immersion for forgiveness of sins, (3) they were the true church of Christ, not a denomination or extension of the Catholic church. They met in homes and consisted of six people to begin with. They were forced to stand in the public market of both Ely and Cambridge nearly naked as punishment for their sins.

In Dover, Kent, in southern England about halfway between London and Calais, France, Lord Cobham had a preacher training school. There were several congregations in Kent, which were in close contact with the church of Christ in Amsterdam Holland, and Colchester, London. Whenever threatened with persecution in one place, those Christians would escape to the other locations until they felt safe enough to return home.

The Broadmead church of Christ was in Bristol in the 1460s. During part of this time, James William, a weaver, preached for the congregation and anyone else who would listen to him. He openly opposed pilgrimages, bowing down to images, and the pope. Later he moved to London where he continued to preach outspokenly, and was finally arrested.

The church of Christ in Wales was known to be in Tewkesbury as well as in Chilterns, the Vale of Evesham, Worcester and other parts of Gloucestershire in the 1100s. At that time people called them Waldensians, but they called themselves just Christians. By the 1400s, people called them Lollards though they, themselves, went by the name church of Christ. Each congregation was autonomous with the leadership of elders. Membership was by immersion baptism of adult believers for forgiveness of their sins.

HOLLAND

Colchester, England, was located about 54 miles from London in one direction, and from Holland in the other direction. During the 15th, 16th, and 17th centuries when persecution of the church was at its height, many members of the church of Christ in Colchester and London escaped to Holland, some returning later if they thought things were safe for a while, and others going on to America.

Along with many others, a sister in Christ, Alice Grevill, was arrested for opposing the Catholic church. She.testified that she had been a member of the church of Christ in Tenterden for twenty-eight years; that is, since 1483.

RUMANIA

In 1405, Nicodim translated the Four gospels into the language of the common people of Rumania. They were located east of the Black Sea near Russia.

BOHEMIA / CZECHOSLOVAKIA

John of Husinec (Huss) in southern Bohemia entered the University of Prague 1390 and became dean of philosophy in 1401. At this time, Bohemia was resisting overbearing influence especially by Germany.

In 1402, he was in charge of the Bethlehem chapel in Prague founded by his teacher, Jan Milic. In 1409, King Wenceslas IV gave tenure to Czech faculty, and foreign scholars complained to Rome. Huss was elected rector of the university.

In 1410, Archbishop Zbynek refused to promote Huss to doctor and Pope Alexander V proclaimed a bull ordering the burning of Wycliffe's works, forbidding further preaching at the Bethlehem chapel. Huss appealed to the pope. Zbynek retaliated by announced his excommunication and burning Wycliffe's books. When he died, Rome took over prosecution of Huss.

In 1412 the sale of indulgences was pushed and Huss objected. Rome excommunicated Huss and the king ordered him to leave Prague.

In 1414 the Council of Constance summoned Huss to defend himself. Upon arrival he was imprisoned. In 1415 he was burned at the stake.

*   *   *   *   *   *   *   *

As was common at this time, anyone who did not identify themselves with the Roman church was named after the person who seemed to be their leader. The followers of Huss were called Hussites.

Vaclav Koranda became their leader after Huss' death. Their basic beliefs were as follows: (1) Open Lord's Supper, both bread and wine given to all Christians; (2) Freedom of preaching from the Scriptures; (4) Poverty of clergy and expropriation of church property; (5) Punishment of notorious sinners, especially prostitutes.

In this same area in Bohemia (Czechoslovakia) Peter Chelcicky led the Hussites until 1460 when he died. Under him, they began to be known as Moravians after the part of Bohemia in which they lived.

Keep in mind that these Christians were struggling to maintain the integrity of the Scriptures in their life at a time when everyone else was telling them they were wrong. They were doing the best they could. Also keep in mind that, although they may have begun pure, future generations may have introduced unscriptural practices. This does not mean they were not originally simple New Testament Christians.

*   *   *   *   *   *   *   *

In the same country, under the leadership of Jan (Johan) Zelivsky, were reformers who felt that even the Moravians had not returned enough to first-century Christianity. His followers were called Bohemian Brethren, emphasizing the intent of the name "church," meaning "the called out ones" or "brethren." He was executed in 1422.

In 1434 these Christians became known as the Bohemian Brethren. After Jan (Johan) Rokycana their next leader was Brother Gregory, who took over in 1457. They began in Prague, but moved to Kunwald.

Their simple Christian teaching, exemplary moral life and industry attracted many. New congregations sprang up needing a minister. So in 1467 in Lhota they met to work out how the New Testament church did things in the days of the apostles.

They knew of the Waldenses and believed they were apostolic and scriptural in their teachings, practices and way of life. Therefore, they asked for leadership from them through Michael Bradacius.

Back in 1447 the Bible began to be printed with movable

type. By now there were thirty-three translations - more help for people who only wanted the simplicity of the first-century New Testament church.

In 1475, the Bible was translated into the Czech language from the Latin, and printed with the new printing press.

In 1499, Gennadius gathered together translations of various books of the Bible into one volume. They had all been translated from the Hebrew, Greek and Latin. It was called the Slavonic Translation of the Bible.

ITALY

In 1471, Nixccolo Malermi translated the Bible into Italian from the Latin translation. It was printed in Venice.

1487, Pope Innocent VIII issued a bull for the extermination of Waldenses in Italy. Alberto de-Capitanei, Archdeacon of Cremona, put himself at the head of this "holy" crusade.

The New Testament church was attacked in Dauphine and Piedmont at the same time. They took refuge in valley of the Angrogne. Charles II, Duke of Piedmont, defended them to save his territory from extinction.

FINLAND

M. Agricola translated the New Testament from the original Greek in the common language of his people, the Finns.

*   *   *   *   *   *   *   *   *   *

During this century, a general term of "Anabaptist" was applied to people who believed in adult baptism only. This term really means re-baptized as an adult after being baptized as a baby. However, this group claimed baptism of a baby was no baptism at all, so rejected the term. In general, they had the following beliefs:

(1)   Baptism of children practiced first by the Catholics

and continued by the classical protestants was unscriptural; (2) Baptism involved repentance, a personal faith, and a pledge to lead a Christian life; (3) Catholic and protestant comparisons of Jewish infant circumcision with Christian infant baptism was nonsense; (4) Original sin and predestination were wrong because Christ's atoning work wiped out the consequences of Adam's fall; therefore infants were not punishable for sin until awareness of good and evil emerged; then they were to exercise their own free will to accept Jesus, personally ask for forgiveness, and be baptized; (5) The church (community of the redeemed) must be separate from the state.

Thousands were martyred by fire and water, declaring no religious organization—whether protestant or Catholic—had authority in the sphere of Christian regeneration, faith and conscience. They opposed use of the sword for social order and war, and refused to swear civil oaths.

The classical/mainline protestants used the local government to implement their reformation. The Anabaptists were not aiming to reform the church. They were determined to restore it in the spirit of the primitive church.

ENDNOTES

[1] . Forbush, William B., Editor, *Fox's Book of Martyrs*, Zondervan Publishing House, Grand Rapids, 1926, pg. 3-5

[2] . Keyes, Nelson B., *Story of the Bible World*, The Reader's Digest Assn., Pleasantville, NY, 1962, pg. 185

[3] . Lightfoot, J. B, Editor, *The Apostolic Fathers*, Baker Book House, Grand Rapids, 1965, pg. 281

[4] . Sisman, Keith, *One Thousand Years of Churches of Christ in England: Traces of the Kingdom*, Forbidden Books Publ., Ramsey, Huntingdon, United Kingdom, 658 pages. And also

https://www.chulavistabooks.com/products/10141-traces-of-the-kingdom/ {From henceforth, unless another source is cited, all future references to the church in Britain are from the research found in this book.}

[5] . Lightfoot, pg. 282-283

[6] . Eusebius, pg. 169

[7] . *Encyclopedia Britannica*, "Waldenses: Sects of the Middle Ages," William Benton, Publisher, Chicago, 1966, Vol. 23, pg. 287-288

BIBLIOGRAPHY

D'Aubigne, J. H. Merle, *History of the Reformation of the Sixteenth Century*, The Religious Tract Society, London, 1846

The Ecclesiastical History of Eusebius Pamphilus, Baker Book House, Grand Rapids, 1971

Encyclopedia Britannica, William Benton Publisher, Chicago, 1966

Forbush, William B., Editor, *Fox's Book of Martyrs*, Zondervan Publishing House, Grand Rapids, 1926

Goold, G. P., Editor, *Bede Historical Works: Ecclesiastical History of the English Nation*, Vol. I and II

Grimm, H. Godwin, *Tradition and History of the Early Churches of Christ In Central Europe,* by Dr. Hans Grimm and Translated by Dr. H. L. Schug, World Evangelism Publications, choate@WorldEvangelism.org, PO Box 72, Winona, MS 38967, USA. It is also on the internet at **http://www.netbiblestudy.net/history**

Keyes, Nelson B., *Story of the Bible World*, Reader's Digest Assn, Pleasantville, NY, 1962

Lightfoot, J.B., Editor, *The Apostolic Fathers*, Baker Book House, Grand Rapids, 1965

McDonald, William J., Editor, *The New Catholic Encyclopedia*, McGraw-Hill, Chicago, 1962

North, James B., *From Pentecost to the Present*, College Press Publishing, Joplin, Mo., 1983

Simon, Edith, *Great Ages of Man: The Reformation*, Time-Life Books, NY, 1968

Burrage, Henry S., [Ana]*Baptist Hymn Writers and their Hymns*, Brown Thurston & Co., Portland, Maine, 1889

Sisman, Keith, *One Thousand Years of churches of Christ in England: Traces of the Kingdom*, ISBN 987-0-9564937-1-2, Forbidden Books Publ., Ramsey, Huntingdon, United Kingdom, 658 pages, 92 photos. **https://www.chulavistabooks .com/products/10141-traces-of-the-kingdom/**

Wells, H. G., *The Outline of History*, Garden City Books, NY, 1961

===

A SPECIAL THANKS TO KEITH SISMAN WHO HAS DONE REMARKABLE RESEARCH OF ANCIENT DOCUMENTS AND LANDMARKS IN ENGLAND AND WALES TO TRACE THE CHURCH OF CHRIST THERE.

5. NEW TESTAMENT-PATTERNED CHURCH

Europe 16th — 18th Centuries

16th Century

This was the century the Catholic church announced that its traditions were as sacred as the Holy Bible and only the Catholic church was allowed to interpret Scriptures.. A chalice of wine must be elevated by the priest so it can better be seen and worshiped. Such things as original sin of babies, necessitating their baptism, were made absolute church law. Sins now were required to be confessed to a priest. It even ordained that choirs were to wear certain kinds of vestments.

BRITAIN

They were not normally demonstrative or heroic, but flourished in quiet evasion. Around 1500 in Kent County alone, congregations were started in Tenderden, Feversham, Maidstone, Canterbury, Eythorne, and Canterbury.

In the Chilterns in 1506 and 1507, forty-five Christians were arrested and prosecuted.

For this search for congregations of the church of Christ, keep in mind that historians often assign names to opponents of the Catholic church that had been given them wrongly by their enemies. One such name continued to be the Lollards. An examination of their beliefs, as recorded by their accusers, show they considered themselves just Christians — no more and no less.

In Essex County, in 1510, some fifty such Christians. were prosecuted. On May 2, 1511, six men and four women were arrested and tried in Kent County near Sevenoaks. They were guilty of (1) Declaring the bread and wine of the Lord's Supper never became the actual body of Christ to be worshiped; (2) Infant baptism and confirmation did the babies no good; (3) No one should confess their sins to a priest since God does not give extra powers such as forgiving sins; (4) Images of "saints" were not to be worshiped or prayed to.

Those arrested were promised their freedom after being tortured if they informed on others with these views. Many were from the Tentarden church of Christ. One husband and two sons witnessed against their wife and mother, Alice Grevill, and she was executed.

In 1514 a New Testament Christian merchant, Richard Hunne was murdered in a church-run prison in St. Paul's. Between 1527 and 1532 at least 218 "heretics" were prosecuted. In 1521, five were burned, and others followed the next decade. Thomas Man was burned at the stake at Smithfield in 1518. All were executed because they just wanted the follow the pattern of the first-century New Testament church.

The Bow Lane church of Christ in London is known to have been meeting as early as the 1520s and possibly earlier. James Bainham and Simon Fish were preachers for this congregation. Before that, they were preachers at the Coleman Street church of Christ.

In 1522, William Tyndale began releasing his translation of the Bible from the original Greek rather than the Latin as his English predecessors had done. He did all of the New Testament. Part of the Old Testament he never finished. He released the entire New Testament in 1526.

In the early 1500s when various groups were trying to break away from the accepted worship established by the Romans, many thought they did not go far enough. They were found later in the various reformation efforts of Lutherans, Methodists, Presbyterians, Congregationalists, Anglicans, Episcopalians and others.

In general they condemned clerical vestments, the sign of the cross, sponsors at baptism, confirmation, observance of church festivals — all relics of the papacy.

Beginning 1525, ten years after Martin Luther began the

Reformation Movement, the churches of Christ said the reformers were not going far enough in such things as autonomous congregations with their own elders and deacons, and use of the Scriptures only as their authority in all things. The term, churches of Christ as being in use is verified by an Anglican theologian, Dr. Fealty who wrote that the "churches of Christ" already existed there in 1525.

In 1529, Simon Fish translated a tract authored by German Henricus Bornelius, and added his own beliefs to it. He named his book "The Sumine of the Holye Scrypture." He taught adult believer's baptism by being "plunged under the water".

Between 1527 and 1532 more than 200 Christians were convicted of heresy against the government-selected church. Half came from London, and half from Colchester, Steeple, Bumstead, Birdbrook and elsewhere in Essex County.

The Coleman Street church of Christ was originally called the Bell Alley church of Christ and probably begun in the 1400s there in London. Among its leaders was John Hacker, who was arrested for distributing books against the Catholic church and for the simple New Testament church at Burford.

Another member of that congregation was John Stacey. Brother Stacey had a man in his house to translate Revelation in English. The man's expenses were paid for by John Sercot, a grocer and another member of the guild.

John Stacey was friends with Lawrence Maxwell, also a Christian. They were both bricklayers and belonged to the guild. Coleman Street was just a brief walk to the Guildhall with members all over England. It was about this time—1530—that the Coleman Street congregation began smuggling Tyndale's New Testament throughout Britain.

In York 32 Christians were prosecuted under King Henry VIII, and 45 under Queen Mary I. The Christians attacked (1) saint worship, (2) images, (3) relics (4) holy bread, (5) holy water, (6) sacred buildings and objects, (7) confession, (8) transubstantiation.

All they wanted was to imitate the simplicity of the New Testament, the first-century New Testament church.

The Bow Lane church of Christ was located in London.

Simon Fish and James Bainham were members. In 1532, Brother Fish was arrested. He declared unabashedly to his accusers that only believers should be baptized in the church of Jesus. On April 20, he was burned at the stake.

Fish's widow married James Bainham. He had been arrested in 1531, and declared in court, "The Truth of the Holy Scriptures" now available to be plainly read by the people since 1526, referring to Tyndale's translation of the Bible into English from Erasmus' Greek. The Bow Lane congregation possibly helped to finance and then smuggle along with the Coleman Street congregation and Canterbury congregation, to other congregations of the Lord's church in Kent. Brother Bainham's torture included the rack, and after enduring several weeks, died by being burned at the stake on April 20, 1532 in the Smithfield district of London.

In 1536 William Tyndale was arrested for heresy in Antwerp, sentenced to death and burned at the stake. Was he a New Testament Christian? Although he was licensed by the Catholic church to preach, it was the only legal way anyone could preach at that time in England. But he did not believe the Catholic doctrines. He wrote that baptism was...

"...the washinge preacheth unto us that we ar clensed with Christe's bloud [blood] shedynge [shedding] which was an offering and a satisfaction for the synn [sin] of al that repent and beleve consentynge [consenting] and submyttyne [submitting] themselves unto the wyl of God. The plungynge into the water sygnyfyeth [signifieth] that we die and are buried with Chryst as concerning ye old life of synne....And the pulling out again sygnyfyeth that we ryse again with Christe in a new lyfeful [life full] of the holye gooste which shal teach us and gyde us, and work the wyll of God in us, as thou seest Rom. 6."

After Tyndale's death, his brother and his brother's children remained faithful. Other relatives, Llewellyn and Hezekiah Tyndale, were members of the church of Christ at Abergaverney, South Wales, near Gloucestershire. Further, Tyndale was friends of the Tracy family who were related to James Bainham, one of the preachers of the Bow Lane congregation in London.

In 1536, *The Great Bible* was edited by Coverdale. Although

German, he was hired by a German Lutheran merchant to do so because he did business in English. Actually, it was a translation of Munster's Latin version of 1535 in the Old Testament and Erasmus' Latin version in the New Testament, the Swiss-German Zurich Bible, Luther's German Bible, and Tyndale's Bible.

By royal decree it was to be installed in every church. It was printed in Paris and nearly finished when the French inquisition intervened. Coverdale and his publisher fled with the types and printed sheets, and completed the printing in London in April 1539.

In 1550, Joan Boucher, a member of the congregation at Eythome, Kent, was burned at the stake on May 2 in Smithfield, London, for helping to smuggle Tyndale's New Testament from London to Kent. She had been friends with Anne Askew, a Christian sister who smuggled a copy of the New Testament into the palace under her skirts.

The church of Christ at Canterbury in Kent was established around 1550.

In the 1100s, autonomous congregations of the Lord's church were generally called Waldenses. Beginning the 1300s, these same groups with the same beliefs began to be called Lollards. Beginning 1538, these same groups with the same beliefs began to be called Anabaptists. Actually, this label was not correct, because it refers to adult believers being baptized again, and members of the church of Christ denied that infant baptism was a real baptism to start with.

William Salesbury translated the New Testament from the original Greek into Welch in 1567. The Bishop's Bible was published in 1568 in English.

In 1588, the Bible was translated by William Morgan into the language of Welch. In some ways it was an offshoot of the Salesbury New Testament translated thirty years earlier. It is used today.

In the 1590s, Bartholomew Legate, along with brothers, Walter and Thomas, preached in congregations around London. They rejected Catholic and church of England rituals. They declared the only person who could be rightly baptized was an adult believer.

Only the locations where the Coleman Street and Bow Lane churches of Christ are known today. There were several congregations in the 1590s as attested to by government records of those they arrested, but their locations today are unknown.

BOHEMIA / CZECHOSLOVAKIA

In 1501, the Bohemian Brethren published the first non-Catholic hymnbook.

Around 1550, many members immigrated to Poland where they began a branch of the Brethren that lasted 200 years.

In 1565, Jan (Johan) Blahoslav translated the New Testament in the Czech language of his people. It was the basis of the later Bible of Kralice published in 1579.

The Bohemian Brethren declared the priesthood of all believers. They were led by elders whom they elected, also called the inner Council. Congregations were under the care only of their own elders. Members were carefully tested as to their sincerity, and their progress in the Christian life was occasionally considered.

They printed their first complete Bible in Czech in 1593, called the Kralice Bible, including Jan Blahoslav's New Testament.

By 1600 half the protesters in Bohemia and over half in adjoining Moravia were of their faith. Many were also in Poland.

SWITZERLAND

Huldreich Zwingli was born 1484 at Wildhaus, Switzerland, and was ordained 1506 at Glarus. Rather than attack the Roman church, he expound the Gospel passages. In 1518, he became known as the people's priest at Grossmunster Cathedral at Zurich. He gave many series of expositions of the New Testament enlivened by topical application.

In 1520, he was given permission by Zurich's governing

Council to preach the "true divine Scriptures" and his sermons stirred revolts against fasting and celibacy.

In 1521 he debated Franz Lambert, declaring the supremacy of Scriptures. In 1522 he published *On Meats* (referring to fasting) and *The Clarity and Certainty of the Word of God*.

He successfully debated celibacy, the liturgy, and in 1524 images. In 1525 all images were removed, organs suppressed, religious houses were dissoluted, the mass was replaced by a simple communion service, baptism was declared for adults only, Bible readings were introduced into the service, and preparation made for a native version of the Bible.

The Zurcher Bible appeared in 1529.

The movement spread from the city of Zurich to nearby towns with the following beliefs:

(1) The church is born of the Word of God and has Christ alone as its head. (2) Its laws are binding only insofar as they agree with Scripture. (3) Christ alone is our righteousness. (4) The Holy Scriptures do not teach Christ's corporeal presence in the bread and wine at the Lord's supper. (5) mass is a gross affront to the sacrifice and death of Christ. (6) There is no biblical foundation for the mediation or intercession of the dead. (7) There is no biblical foundation for purgatory. (8) There is no biblical foundation for images and pictures. (9) Marriage is lawful to all.

In 1525, Zwingly wrote *On Baptism*, emphasizing the significance of water baptism as a covenant sign. In 1531 he wrote *Tricks of the Catabaptists*.

In 1525, Conrad Grebel, a Zwinglian in Switzerland, believed Zwingli was cooperating too much with the government. His followers believed in: (1) Separation of church and state; (2) Voluntarism in matters of faith; (3) Believer's baptism; (4) Pacifism; (5) Rejection of oaths

They became known as Swiss Brethren. They were persecuted, so fled to Alsace in south Germany and into Austria where the Hutterian Brethren had been meeting.

The Bible was translated in 1560 into the language of Swiss, and published in Geneva. It was called the Upper Engadine Translation of the Bible and done by J. Bifrun from the Vulgate into this Romanish Swiss dialect.

FRANCE

In 1523, Jacques Lefevre translated the New Testament from Latin to French. In 1530 he released the Old Testament.

In 1534, Olivetan translated the Bible into the language of the French from the Hebrew, Erasmus' Latin version, and Lefevre's New Testament. More and more people were given the opportunity to become Christians in the simple way, the first-century New Testament way.

AUSTRIA

In 1528 in Austria, Jakob Hutter, a Tirolean, led his Hutterian Brethren in like beliefs of the New Testament church, following the New Testament exclusively in its first-century pattern. He was burned as a heretic in 1536.

NETHERLANDS

In 1532 Luther's German Bible was translated into Dutch. That is all they needed to establish the New Testament church after the simple New Testament pattern.

In 1534, simultaneously in the Netherlands, Obbe Philips led people to believe the same. In 1536, Philips baptized a Roman Catholic priest who just wanted to be a Christian like people were in New Testament days.

GERMANY

Grimm explained in his book that, despite the Catholic church's crusades against non-conformers, "Even in these dark ages, the churches of Christ did not only hold their ground in their strongholds in Alsace-Lorraine, Switzerland, and the Netherlands, but from 1518 to 1538 they succeeded in multiplying their congregations in the Palatinate, Austria, Moravia, and in the center of Germany."

By 1524, there were some 12,000 baptized Christians in Alsace-Lorraine, 5,000 in the Palatinate, 2,500 in Frisia, and 2,000 in Salzburg. The Catholic church basically went to war against all those independent congregations that refused to fall under their authority.

Martin Luther translated the New Testament from the original Greek into common German and published it in 1526. In 1534 he translated the Old Testament from the original Hebrew.

A number of fleeing Waldenses ended up in Germany where they found refuge. They influenced, and afterward joined, the Hussites and the Bohemian Brethren who had been independently re-establishing the New Testament church in their own regions, based only on the New Testament. Remember, these were names given them by their enemies.

The Dutch Mennonites early in the century had spread into the Rhineland, across north Germany to the delta of the Vistula River in the Danzig area, and became more numerous than the Swiss and South German Anabaptists.

In 1530, Georges Morel of Dauphine, and Pierre Masson of Provence conferred with German and Swiss Reformers. An extant letter to Oecolampadius shows their attempt to separate from all organized religion and form only the New Testament church.

They were even disturbed, not only about Catholic doctrines, but also about the Lutheran and Calvinistic teaching against freewill and pro-predestination (irresistible salvation).

At first they continued to submit to baptism and communion from Catholic priests, but then isolated themselves for their own secret services. They finally broke away completely.

The Waldenses in 1532 at Chanforans in the valley of the Angrogne, then merged with the Swiss and German reformers. They renounced all future recognition of Rome, and decided to worship in public.

In 1534 J. Dietenberger translated the Bible into the

language of the German people from the Latin. He also used Emser's New Testament and Luther's Old Testament

The Dutch Mennonites early in the century had spread into the Rhineland, across north Germany to the delta of the Vistula River in the Danzig area, and became more numerous than the Swiss and South German Anabaptists.

Grimm, writing of the Catholic war on "heretics" who refused to submit to their authority, said, "The result of this decree was the almost total extermination of the churches of Christ in Alsace-Lorraine, Switzerland, the Palatinate, and Central Germany. With about 100,000 Anabaptists, more than 42,000 followers of Christ were given their choice between revocation and mounting the pyre. By far the greater number chose the latter. Under the witnesses for the gospel truth were four of my ancestors: Agustine and Adolf Grimm in 1525, Godwin Engel in 1535, and the younger Gregor Cron in 1536."

By the end of the century, the churches of Christ basically ceased to exist in Germany, not only due to the persecution by the Catholic church, but also the Lutherans and Calvinists. John Calvin voted to burn at the stake Michael Servetus in Geneva, Switzerland, 1541. Lutheran theologian, Melanchthon, supported the burning, drowning and beheading of over 1,000 baptized members of the church in Thuringen and Saxony.

But, as always seems to be the case, a hidden remnant remained. Some 1,000 existed in the Vosges Mountains of Alsace-Lorainne and swamps of Frisia. A few congregations in Hesse and Tyrol were protected by a few Hussite noblemen in Moravia.

DENMARK

In 1528, Christiern Pedersen translated the New Testament from two different Latin versions and Luther's German version into the language of his people, Danish.

ITALY

In 1532, Antonio Brucioli translated the Bible into the language of the common people of Italy, using Erasmus' Latin version for the New Testament, and Pagninus' Latin version for the Old Testament.

Although the Waldenses had the New Testament and part of the Old printed in their language, they wanted the complete Bible. They furnished a Swiss printer with the entire Old and New Testament who accommodated them.

HUNGARY

In 1541, J. Erdosi translated the New Testament from the original Greek into the Hungarian language. Yes, regardless of whether or not they were registered with a world headquarters in heaven, they had every opportunity to begin the New Testament church the way the apostles set it up in the New Testament.

SPAIN

In 1543, Enzinas Dryander translated the New Testament from the original Greek in the common language of the Spanish. What a movement of getting the Bible into the hands of the people so they could read for themselves!

HOLLAND

Around 1525, Menno Simons, a priest at Pingjum in Holland began studying Luther's tracts and to study the New Testament and to question infant baptism. In 1531 the tailor Sicke Freerks was executed for having been rebaptized as a believing adult. Simons moved to Witmarsum and briefly identified with Munster's Anabaptists. In 1536 he left the Roman church. Within a year he became a minister for the Obbenites led by Obbe Philips.

When Obbe Philips left the group, Menno took over as leader. He repudiated the idea that he had formed a sect. He said that any who had experienced the "new birth" were the true Christian church. He did not take to the term Trinity since it was not in the Bible, and he believed the flesh of Christ had its origin from God rather than Mary.

He moved around, starting congregations often. He was in East Friesland until 1541; Amsterdam, North Holland until 1542; back to East Friesland until 1545; then Lubeck, South Holland until 1547; Wismar until 1554; Wustenfelde until he died in 1561. From his name came the term Mennonite, though he disliked it, preferring simply the church of Christ.

In 1554, the New Testament was translated into the language of the Dutch based on Erasmus' Greek text of the New Testament.

RUSSIA

In 1579 thousands of these Dutch Mennonites fled from Prussia to south Russia and settled in the Ukraine German-speaking colonies where they flourished. The Swiss-German Mennonites settled in the Ukraine also. These Dutch-Russian Mennonites and Swiss-German Mennonites then united in the Ukraine.

The Mennonite worship originally involved what Christians did in the first century. (1) Congregational singing with no musical instruments; (2) Ministers preaching sermons based entirely on the Bible; (3) Worshipers kneeling for prayer.

Again, the reminder that, although a group began as a replica of the New Testament church, changes occurred in later generations.

EASTERN EUROPE

In 1550, J. Seklucyan published the New Testament in the Danish language from the original Greek. In 1553, he translated the New Testament into the Polish from the original Greek. It was the first one published with the new printing press.

The Cracow Bible was the first entire Bible published in Polish, and was translated from the Latin in 1561.

Coresi translated the Acts of the Apostles from earlier manuscripts written during the Huss movement to the Romanian language.

In 1590, G. Karoli translated the Bible into the language of his people, Hungary, from the original Greek and Hebrew.

Why are these translations important? Because, every time they appeared, a new rebellion arose against the large and growing Catholic, Lutheran, and Calvinist churches, and in favor of going all the way back to the beginning with the New Testament church of Christ.

17th Century

Candles were now required to be burned at mass (the Lord's Supper), yet another adoption from the old Law of Moses. All laws of the church were enforced by governments which wanted the favor and wealth of the growing powerful Catholic church.

BRITAIN

Edward Wightman and Bartholomew Legate were anti-Trinitarians. The Nicene Creed was originated with the Catholic church. It was rejected by the churches of Christ. In 1611, they declared "There is one God, the best and highest and most glorious Creator and Preserver of all; who is Father, Son, and Holy Spirit." Later in 1646 they explained, "The Lord our God is but one God, whose subsistence is in Himself; whose essence cannot be comprehended by any but himself, who only hath immortality, dwelling in the light, which no man can approach unto; who is in Himself most holy....In this divine and infinite Being there is the Father, the Word and the Holy Spirit; each having the whole divine

Essence undivided; all infinite without any beginning and therefore but one God; who is not to be divided in nature, and being, but distinguished by several peculiar relative properties."

In 1611, Bartholomew and his brother, Thomas, both preachers in the London area, were arrested for heresy and imprisoned. Thomas died in Newgate Prison, and Bartholomew was burned to death at the stake in the Smithfield section of London, March 18, 1612.

On December 14, 1611, our Brother Edward Wightman, a member of the Burton-Upon-Trent church of Christ was convicted of heresy for being a member of this autonomous congregation instead of the church of England, being against infant baptism, and declaring the Lord's Supper and baptism as kept by the Catholic church and church of England were not correct. His sentence read, "holding that such a heritick in the aforesaid form convicted and condemned according to the customs and laws of this our Kingdom of England in this part accustomed....being in thy custody to be committed to fire in some publick and open place before the city aforesaid...for the manifest example of other Christians that they may not fall into the same crime." He was burned to death at the stake April 11,1612 at Lichfield. He was the last Christian to be condemned to the flames in Britain.

His widow and orphaned children moved to London where they attended the church of Christ at White Alley in Newgate. Later they moved to Rhode Island in America where they continued to worship with the church of Christ there.

There was a congregation in Amsterdam that immigrated to London around 1612. At first, they met at the Spittlefields district of London. Soon thereafter, they moved to the Newgate section at London Bridge, and from then on was known as the Newgate church of Christ.

One of the members, Thomas Helwys, was arrested and died in prison in 1616. One of Thomas' friends was John Murton who he had met ten years earlier. John was an elder and preacher for the Newgate church of Christ. In one of his pamphlets that still exists today, he said this:

"Members and churches of Christ, are so made both by faith

and baptism, and not by the one only, which being true; it will follow, that neither the church and members of Rome, are members of the church of Christ, because Faith is neither required nor performed thereto; nor yet any profession of people, that separate from Rome as no church of Christ, retaining Rome's baptism, and building new churches without baptism." He used Romans 11:20f as his proof text.

The Newgate congregation met half a mile from the Bell Alley congregation and two miles from the Southwark congregation, all in London. There were undoubtedly more.

In the 1620s, congregations in Britain were in London, Lincoln, Epworth, Sarum in Salisbury, Coventry, Tiverton in Devon, Warrington at Hill Cliff, Plymouth, Amersham, Olchon in Wales, Stoney Stratford, Eyethom and Monks-Thorpe.

In 1620, the *Mayflower* landed in America with several members of the Bell Alley and Southwark in London churches of Christ. The captain of the Mayflower, Christopher Jones, was from Southwark.

Thomas Lamb was a preacher for the Bell Alley congregation (known later as the Coleman Street church of Christ) in London. He was arrested in 1640 and released on bail with the warning "not to preach, baptize or frequent any [unlawful church assemblies]". Lamb traveled around western Britain preaching in private homes and baptizing. "By preaching there, he subverted many, and shortly afterward in an extreme cold and frosty time in the night season, diverse men and women were rebaptized in the great River Severn, in the City of Gloucester." Lamb had a son, Isaac, who became a preacher at the East Smithfield church of Christ in London, a congregation of some 300 people!

The Broadmead church of Christ in Bristol, was founded in 1640. John Tombes was their preacher, and tried to reform the church of England, and a sermon was printed in the record of the House of Commons. Possibly as a result, in 1642, he fled to Bristol, and finally to London.

In 1645, Brother Tombes learned of problems of the churches of Christ in New England, America, regarding infant baptism, and wrote them to teach them further and encourage them.

Benjamin Cox was preacher for the church of Christ at Bedford. He was the son of an Anglican bishop. In 1643 he was jailed in Coventry for preaching against infant baptism.

The church of Christ at Southwark in London was organized around 1621. The first preacher was Mr. Hubbard or Herbert, and the second was John Canne. From there, Canne started the Broadmead congregation in Bristol.

In 1642, famous Anglican theologian, Dr. Daniel Featley, debated four members of the Southwark congregation in London, then published a book about it in 1645 called *The Dippers dipt or the Anabaptists dunckt and plunged over head and ears.* It is from his opposition to the churches of Christ that we learn of their beliefs at that time.

In 1641, Henry Denne, preached a sermon at Baldock based on John 5:35, trying to reform the church of England. He was taught further by Thomas Lamb, the preacher of the Bell Alley church of Christ in London, then resigned from the church of England. He began traveling around England preaching and establishing congregations in the counties of Staffordshire, Cambridgeshire, Huntingdonshire, Lincoln-shire, Kent and elsewhere. He was occasionally arrested. In 1646 he was arrested at Spalding in Lincolnshire for preaching baptism by immersion.

In 1646 in Spalding, Henry Denne preached in the home of merchant, John Makernesse and converted four people: Anne Stennet, Anne Croft, Godfrey Root and John Sowter. They decided to be baptized at midnight in the Little Croft to avoid detection. But word got out and Denne was arrested in Lincoln goal.

Later in 1646 Oliver Cromwell convinced Parliament to reverse their policy so that such independent congregations were not treasonous. In fact, Cromwell's daughter married a New Testament Christian. So Denne was released, then preached and started churches of Christ at Rochester, Chatham, Canterbury, Ely, Eltisly, St. Ives, Spalding, Warboys, and Whittlesey.

In 1650, Henry Denne and others started a congregation in St. Ives, Huntingdonshire (Cambridgeshire). His son, John, continued that work after Henry's death. In 1655, Denne gave up his missionary work and became the minister of the Fenstanton church of Christ at Canterbury.

Over in Bristol, the extant Broadmead church records say, "God brought to this city one Mr. Canne, a baptized man. It was Mr. Canne that made notes and references upon the Bible." The wife of a local priest, Mrs. Hazzard, invited Canne to her home where he taught the difference between the Catholic church and the church of Christ. This is how the congregation started.

About 1640, Bro. Cann stated in a pamphlet that there were "many thousands in England that doe not hold communion with others, though they doe owne and practise believers' baptism, because they hold with it free will and falling from grace".

In 1651, Brother Ewins became the Broadmead, Bristol, preacher. In addition to meeting on the Lord's day, they met on Thursday evenings in private homes to discuss Scriptures and fellowship each other. Robert Purnell was one of the elders.

At first, they met at Friars Chapel under the protection of Oliver Cromwell who believed in relative freedom of religion. When Cromwell died, they met in private homes. Regardless, they were often discovered, arrested and imprisoned until they could pay a fine. If they learned ahead of time the authorities were coming, they would hide in a cellar or attic.

In 1661, Brother Ewins was arrested while preaching, and again in 1663. He was imprisoned on the fourth floor of the jail. On Sundays he would preach from the window.

Their records of 1665 say, "We had many disturbances and divers imprisoned, but the Lord helped us through it." Further, if anyone missed worship out of fear, the members considered them "disorderly". But persecution grew until "we were fain to meet in the lanes and highways for several months."

In 1658, persecution of Christians by the church of England began again. That same year, Roger Sawrey of London traveled to today's English Lake District in Cumberland Shire. He met two Anglican clergymen who were dissatisfied, William Campbell and George Malcom. At the time there were already two churches of Christ meeting in Cumberland, one in Broughton (begun in 1648) and one in Cockermouth (begun in 1641). These two congregations were forced to cease meeting, but later merged and, in 1662, began the Tottlebank and Wall End churches of Christ. At that time, there was also a congregation in Tavistock in Devonshire.

One of the debaters of the author of *The Dippers dipt or the Anabaptists dunckt and plunged over head and ears* was William Cuffin/Kiffin who preached at Devonshire Square. He had been baptized in 1639 and was a wealthy London merchant and friend of King Charles II. In 1664 he rescued twelve Christians who had been sentenced to death for participating in an illegal church.

In 1667 the Broadmead congregation in Bristol moved to the second story of a large warehouse. Their minister, Brother Ewin, died in April 1670, and the authorities broke up a worship service, arresting some of the members and demanding fines. In 1671, Thomas Hardcaster became their preacher.

In 1672, King Charles II allowed "dissenters" to preach and hold meetings, but this new freedom only lasted a year. During that time, the St. Ives church of Christ in Cambridgeshire met in a chapel, part of a bridge over the Ouse River.

In 1678, our Brothers Ward and Blenkinsop started a congregation at Hawkshead Hill of Furness-fells in Lancashire.

The years 1682 and 1683 saw the church ravaged throughout Britain. Congregations of the church of Christ met in homes, fields, woods, or any other hiding place they could find.

POLAND

Although the church in Poland remained stable, in 1618 the Thirty Years War broke out with the Catholics, and in 1627, leading nobles who had become protestants were beheaded and Protestantism was banned.

All the Brethren church buildings, Bibles and hymnbooks were destroyed, and it members forced to be Catholic or be forever exiled. They no longer existed as a single body of individual congregations known to each other.

But they did continue to exist, each in secret meetings in the forests. Among them was Bishop Johann [Jan] Amos Comenius

[Komensky] who lived in the northern countries and wrote, collected money for sufferers, publicly appealed for religious liberty which can only come about through common education of everyone.

He moved easily among denominations, trying to bring them together, but this irritated many. He forever hoped that there might lie a "hidden seed" from which to renew a large body of Brethren. It happened in Germany.

The Mennonites were one such Anabaptist group. Another sprang up in Holland. Fleeing from Poland in the 1600s, the Socinians introduced their practice of baptism by immersion in their new country. It was adopted by the Arminian Collegiants.

At that time, the English General Baptists were living there, having been exiled from England and its Anglican church. The practice of immersion was taken over by these Baptists in their midst.

AMERICAN COLONY

As mentioned in the account of Britain, in late 1611, Edward Wightman, a member of the Burton-Upon-Trent church of Christ was convicted of heresy and was burned at the stake in early 1612 at Lichfield.

His widow and orphaned children moved to London where they attended the church of Christ at White Alley in Newgate. Later they moved to Rhode Island in America where they continued to worship with the church of Christ there.

In 1620, the *Mayflower* landed in America with several members of the Bell Alley and Southwark in London churches of Christ. The captain of the Mayflower, Christopher Jones, was from Southwark. Many passengers kept their ties with the church of England. But, within a few years, several of the other passengers separated and established the church of Christ.

The Broadmead church of Christ in Bristol, was founded in 1640. John Tombes was their preacher.

In 1645, Tombes learned of problems of the churches of Christ in New England, America, regarding infant baptism, and wrote them to teach them further and encourage them. Brother Emlin, a minister of one of the churches of Christ in Boston and one other town, insisted on believer baptism. His letter mentioned that they were evangelizing Indians. At least one congregation was established within the Indian community in Massachusetts in the 1640s.

On May 28, 1665, a congregation from England was formed in Boston. They called themselves "Baptists", this being before that denomination began, only trying to identify their belief in adult baptism.

18th Century

Mary was declared as the intercessoress between man and her Son, Jesus, and was the one who granted all favors. The reasoning was that Jesus was more likely to listen to his mother than common Christians on earth.

BRITAIN

In 1727, Thomas Lamb, preacher for the Bell Alley congregation in London, began preaching for the Bow Lane congregation, also in London.

In 1742, William Whitson, colleague of John Newton of science fame, was baptized for forgiveness of his sins. Ten years earlier, he translated *Josephus*. He lived in Rutlandshire where several congregations of the church of Christ existed.

The first congregation of Moravian Brethren New Testament church was established in London. From there they branched out to Yorkshire, Wiltshire and Ireland. John Cennick was their most powerful evangelist.

In 1749, the English parliament officially recognized the Moravian church "as an ancient protestant episcopal church" and gave these Christians colonization privileges. The congregations always remained small because of their emphasis in dividing up and sending missionaries out from them.

By 1768, some 200,000 people died in witch hunts. Even reformers under Luther and Calvin supported it. The guide was always the same: If a witch practiced Mark 16:16, s/he was guilty of demon possession. John Wesley stated in 1768, "Giving up witchcraft was, in effect, giving up the Bible".

In 1791, the congregation of the church of Christ at Morcott obtained a baptistry from Greetham.

GERMANY

In 1722, Count Zinzendorf allowed the Moravian Brethren to move onto his estate at Herrnhut Saxony. Several German Lutherans joined them. The count came to live with them and organize it according to the original beliefs of the Brethren and the New Testament pattern of the New Testament church.

In 1732, they decided missions was everyone's responsibility. Missionaries were sent to Russia, Egypt, Germany, Switzerland, Holland, Scandinavia, West Indies, and Georgia in the United States. They called their missionary work "diaspora" after the dispersion mentioned in 1 Peter 1:1, brethren ministering among the "scattered" everywhere.

Grimm, in his history of the New Testament church in Europe, concluded, "The small churches in Alsace-Lorraine had to endure their last persecution during the great French Revolution (1789-99). Here died the last three martyrs, beheaded as "anti-revolutionists" at Colmar under the terror reign of the former Roman Catholic priest, Eulogius Schneider.

He concluded, "The small congregation of the church of my ancestors in Alsace-Lorraine and other scattered churches in Poland, Ukraine, and Siberia, which remained through the centuries in close connection with one another, claimed to be the true church of Christ."

SCOTLAND

In the 17th century in Scotland, protestant John Dury was wholly consecrated to the ideal of the unity of the church. He traveled tirelessly, attempting to influence leaders in all denominations to unite. He preached, he wrote, he argued, he dedicated his life to this.

Scotland had long been frustrated by monarchs coming out of England, especially those legislating their religion. By the 18th century, there were divisions primarily in the Presbyterian church based on how much control the government should have over them.

In 1728 John Glas became an Independent Congregationalist, followers were called Glasites, adopted immersion of adult believers. About 1755, Robert Sandeman took over leadership of this independent group. (Keep in mind, independent religious groups were normally called by the name of their primary leader by outsiders.)

In 1749, John Erskinbe published his "Essay to Promote the More Frequent Dispensation of the Lord's Supper", eliminating all the extra days such as Lent, and instead, celebrating it every Sunday. Dr. John Mason agreed, and was sent as a missionary to America in 1761. His son, Dr. John Mason, preached and wrote the same beliefs.

In the mid-1760s, David Dale, father-in-law of the famous Robert Owen who first showed compassion on workers in factories, became independent and adopted weekly communion. In 1769, they built a meeting house, appointed elders, and became an independent congregation.

In 1773, a Dr. Johnson, decided Christianity should be based exclusively upon the Bible, and eventually went out to be a missionary of religious reform.

A congregation of the Lord's church was established in Glasgow at Morrison's Court around 1775. By 1818, they had 180 members. A congregation of the church of Christ was established in Kirkcaldy in the middle 1780s. In 1798 they rented a meeting place at Kirk Wynd. In 1819, they built the Rose Street Chapel with a seating capacity of 200. A congregation was established at Leith Walk in Edinburgh around 1798. By 1818, they had 250 members.

In 1786, William Jones author of the *History of the Waldenses*, was immersed at Chester. He then returned to London, England.

Around 1793 in Rich Hill, the Haldane brothers began

questioning church laws that were not borne out in Scripture. They adopted the Wesleyan system of lay-preaching and field preaching since the officially recognized clergy were hostile to their teaching the people what was in the Bible.

In 1798 James Haldane and others organized the Society for Propagating the Gospel, but remained in the church of Scotland. They insisted on evidence from the Bible for all things; without evidence there can be no faith (Hebrews 11:1 KJV). The following year they were excommunicated from the church of Scotland. They formed a congregational church.

Under the leadership of a Mr. Ewing, they began keeping the Lord's Supper every Sunday. Under the teaching of William Ballantine, they began having congregational elders as their only form of rule. Under James Haldane, they ceased baptizing children; and shortly after began preaching immersion of believing adults.

The Haldanes regarded preaching Christ crucified as the great essential, and wished all differences about church order and ordinances to be matters of forbearance. Other ministers adopted these views—a Mr. Innes of Edinburgh, William Stevens of Edinburgh Seminary, a Dr. Carson, and Archibald McLean.

A Mr. Barclay founded a group called the Bereans, so called after the example of the church in Berea who "searched the Scriptures daily" (Acts 17:11).

AMERICAN COLONY

Further tracing of the New Testament church ceases here, except to briefly show how, as congregations of the church of Christ in Europe faded away, the torch was picked up elsewhere. This time it was in America.

Again, this is a difficult task because people wishing to follow only the New Testament pattern were not organized beyond the congregational level. God knew who they were, but we do not always. It will be noted that many of the people in America who preached independence and following only the New

Testament pattern were Scottish.

In 1790, a popular Presbyterian minister, James McGready in North Carolina, began preaching that congregations should be independent and should have only the Bible as its creed.

In 1793 in North Carolina and Virginia, James O'Kelly and some other Methodist preachers pleaded for a congregational system and that the New Testament be the only creed and discipline. Unable to convince their episcopate to abide by this, they seceded.

James O'Kelly's group left their denomination at Manakin Town, North Carolina, in December of that year. At first they took the name "Republican Methodists," but later resolved to be known as Christians only and to acknowledge no head but Christ, and have no creed or discipline but the Bible.

Not long afterward, unknown to the groups in North Carolina and Virginia, up in Vermont Abner Jones, a Baptist, became greatly dissatisfied with sectarian names and creeds. He pleaded that these should be abolished. In September 1800, Abner Jones of Hartland, Vermont, seceded from their denomination and began meeting at Lyndon, Vermont. That group had 25 members. In 1803, he helped another congregation form at Pierpont, New Hampshire.

About that same time, not knowing about the others, a Baptist preacher named Elias Smith of Portsmouth, New Hampshire, influenced his congregation to secede and become an independent congregation of believers. Several other ministers, both from the Regular and the Freewill Baptists, soon after followed. Then others rose up all over the New England States, New York, Pennsylvania, Ohio and Canada. They, too, went only by the name "Christian."

Another movement, unbeknownst to the others, began down in Kentucky under the influence of a Presbyterian preacher, Barton Warren Stone, who in earlier years had also been a Baptist and a Methodist. In 1801 Stone went to Logan County, Kentucky, to hear James McGready, visiting there from North Carolina.

Upon returning home to Cane Ridge, Kentucky, he preached the same thing. In August he held an outdoor meeting where more than 20,000 people attended. Methodist and Baptist preachers aided, several preaching in different parts at the same time.

Among other preachers led into the Bible-only movement were Presbyterians by the name of McNamar, Thompson, Dunlavy, Marshall, and David Purviance. The Synod at Lexington then suspended them and declared their congregations vacant.

At first, these independent congregations formed what they called the Springfield Presbytery, but later they decided it was unscriptural, so disbanded it, agreeing to take the name only of Christian. If anyone wanted to call their congregations by a name, they insisted it be the "Christian Connection."

In 1808, some 150 years after the first-known New Testament Christians arrived in the New World, Thomas Campbell arrived in Pennsylvania from Scotland. He had been a Presbyterian preacher all his life; his father and grandfather had been Roman Catholics. Campbell was given a church to preside over in Pennsylvania.

In 1809 he was denounced by the Associate Synod of North America for preferring to discard their rules in order to bring people of all faiths together.

Thereupon, he reported to his congregation what happened, and they decided to cede with him. He then admonished them to have only one rule: "That rule, my highly respected hearers is this, that where the Scriptures speak, we speak; and where the Scriptures are silent, we are silent."

He then went on to say that, "Whatever private opinions might be entertained upon matters not clearly revealed must be retained in silence, and no effort must be made to impose them upon others....Simply, reverentially, confidingly, all will speak of Bible things in Bible words, adding nothing thereto and omitting nothing given by inspiration."

They named themselves "The Christian Association." The Campbell biographer said "The idea that he should...be the means of creating a new party [denomination] was most abhorrent to the mind of Thomas Campbell." Thomas continued to inspire others to exist in independent congregations, influencing thousands over the next 40 years.

His son, Alexander, also became a minister of the simple Gospel, declaring the Bible the only possible creed of a Christian. Although he was no more important than any other Christian leader, he was editor of a Christian periodical and publicly debated all religious leaders, and even one famous atheist, so was more widely known than some of the others.

He became personal friend to Presidents James Buchanan and William Harrison, as well as Henry Clay, Secretary of State under President John Adams. He was the only minister ever to speak before both Houses of the U.S. Congress. And whenever preaching in the Washington D.C. area, many congressmen went to hear him. He and Barton W. Stone also influenced the beliefs of President Abraham Lincoln from Kentucky and Illinois.

By 1860, it was estimated that there were some half million people in North America embracing the restoration movement of being simple New Testament Christians.

Conclusion

What does it take to be the original New Testament church? Not a succession. It happens by producing carbon copies, or as we say today, photocopies of the original. All we have to do to see if we're the original New Testament church is hold up the Mirror, the New Testament. Is it a perfect image?

The "mainline" reformation denominations obtained status by being recognized by their national governments. For example....

Lutherans - National Religion of Germanic nations
Episcopalians - National Religion of England
Presbyterians - National Religion of Scotland
Calvinists – National Religion of Switzerland
Reformed churches - National Religion of Holland

Such "mainline" denominations as these claim the largest numbers today. However, when combining all the smaller groups with the desire to restore the New Testament church rather than try to reform it, their numbers are quite high.

It is impossible to tell who all the groups are today who have these beliefs. In talking with many people in many denominations, there is a wide number of people in them all who interpret the Scriptures more literally than they are taught by their leaders. For example, the author's experience finds that most believe baptism is necessary but are not sure why, they like the idea of having the Lord's Supper every Sunday, they believe in a plurality of elders and that they be men, and they wouldn't miss the piano if it were discarded in their worship. But, they do not know which other congregations believe as they do. "They can't find us. So they either stay put or quit going to church anywhere."

However, some of those who do agree in most points are [using 1990 U.S. stastistics] churches of Christ, (1,800,000) Disciples of Christ (144,000), Christian church (40,000), Brethren (206,000), and Mennonite (302,000) churches. These total nearly 2,500,000 putting them as a group in the top seven protestant groups in the U.S. which, at least at the beginning, desired to restore the original New Testament church of Christ. Add Christians giving either no denomination or protestants giving no denomination and that is another 2,500,000, giving this group a possible 5,000,000. And add to that Christians identifying themselves with mainline churches because they do not know where to go, that brings the potential number even higher.

Does this mean compromise in order to unite? No. Does it mean adding a few embellishments so we're more popular? No. Does it mean not mentioning doctrine so we can pretend we are united in Christ? No. It means working together to go forward, back to the original New Testament church!

BIBLIOGRAPHY

D'Aubigne, J. H. Merle, *History of the Reformation of the Sixteenth Century*, The Religious Tract Society, London, 1846

The Ecclesiastical History of Eusebius Pamphilus, Baker Book House, Grand Rapids, 1971

Encyclopedia Britannica, William Benton Publisher, Chicago, 1966

Forbush, William B., Editor, *Fox's Book of Martyrs,* Zondervan Publishing House, Grand Rapids, 1926

Goold, G. P., Editor, *Bede Historical Works: Ecclesiastical History of the English Nation,* Vol. I and II

Grimm, H. Godwin, *Tradition and History of the Early Churches of Christ In Central Europe,* by Dr. Hans Grimm and Translated by Dr. H. L. Schug, World Evangelism Publications, choate@WorldEvangelism.org, PO Box 72, Winona, MS 38967, USA. It is also on the internet at **http://www.netbible studynet/history**

Keyes, Nelson B., *Story of the Bible World*, Reader's Digest Assn, Pleasantville, NY, 1962

Lightfoot, J.B., Editor, *The Apostolic Fathers,* Baker Book House, Grand Rapids, 1965

McDonald, William J., Editor, *The New Catholic Encyclopedia*, McGraw-Hill, Chicago, 1962

North, James B., *From Pentecost to the Present,* College Press Publishing, Joplin, Mo., 1983

Simon, Edith, *Great Ages of Man: The Reformation,* Time-Life Books, NY, 1968

Burrage, Henry S., [Ana]*Baptist Hymn Writers and their Hymns*, Brown Thurston & Co., Portland, Maine, 1889

Sisman, Keith, *One Thousand Years of churches of Christ in England:*

Traces of the Kingdom, ISBN 987-0-9564937-1-2, Forbidden Books Publ., Ramsey, Huntingdon, United Kingdom, 658 pages, 92 photos Also **https://www. chulavistabooks.com/products/10141-traces-of-the-kingdom/**

Wells, H. G., *The Outline of History,* Garden City Books, NY, 1961

6. FORWARD! BACK TO THE FIRST CENTURY!

Divided We Fall!

A chapter for our denominational friends

> *God, you alone are worthy of praise – Father of Life, Spirit of Promise, Son of Glory. We fall at your feet unworthy of your love and your notice. We are sinners. Yet you love us still.*

There was a young lady in high school a long time ago who sometimes got a little "into herself". Occasionally she would get out her mirror, flick a willowy wisp of hair back, and say to the mirror, "You gorgeous doll, you! I can hardly stand myself sometimes, I'm so gorgeous! Look at what you've done for the world; your beauty is beyond belief! Oh, you gorgeous, doll!"

Well, as long as she didn't do it every day, we thought it was kind of funny. Funny because she didn't really believe it. If, for a second we thought she did believe it, we would have walked away from her in disgust. Besides, although she was attractive, she wasn't knock-out gorgeous. Of course, if she had been, her talking to her mirror like that would have turned us off too.

But isn't that what we have done in the religious world today? Haven't individual denominations been flaunting how wonderful we are in front of others? And meaning it?

Who is perfect? Only God is perfect. How dare we flaunt our perfection in front of God? How dare we flaunt our perfection in front of each other and create division in the church!

Only one thing can bring unity, and that is to "flaunt" our sinful state in front of each other. Then together we must all kneel at the cross in humiliation and beg Jesus to forgive our pride.

Our divisiveness is one of the reasons people have left the

church completely. Our divisiveness is one of the reasons we cannot attract lost souls. Our divisiveness does not bless us, but rather curses us. It gets us sidetracked from the real issue of saving souls.

When Jesus' apostles discovered some stranger casting out demons in Christ's name, they said, "we told him to stop, because he was not one of us." What did Jesus reply?

"Do not stop him! No one who does a miracle in my name can in the next moment say anything bad about me, for whoever is not against us is for us"(Mark 9:38-40). [1]

What is also interesting about this is that the complaint came from a spirit of pride. A few days prior to this event, Jesus found his apostles arguing. Why? They had all taken their turn trying to cast out a demon, but all failed (Mark 9:16, 28f). Could it be they were arguing over whose fault it was that their miracle didn't work?

Then, on down the road, they started arguing yet again! This time it was over who was going to be greatest when Jesus set up his new kingdom (Mark 9:33-35)!

Still not having learned their lesson, even after Jesus told them, "Do not stop them," they began excluding children from coming to Jesus (Mark 10:13-16)! This self-elevation made Jesus "indignant" at them.

And if that weren't enough, James and John returned to him with their mother wanting to be "cardinal" and "vice-cardinal" in the new kingdom (Mark 10:35-38)!

They were still thinking in terms of an earthly kingdom and an earthly headquarters (probably in Jerusalem).

If this is what the prospect of world headquarters on earth did to the closest friends of Jesus himself, what has it done to us today?

Every once in a while someone knocks on my door wishing to tell me about Jesus and his love for me. Occasionally one of them will ask me what my denominational affiliation is. When I answer, "I'm just a Christian," they reply, "But what kind of Christian?". When I reply, "just a Christian of the Bible," they say, "Oh, you belong to the Christ of the Bible church?" Then I reply something like, "No, I'm just a Christian who belongs to the church of the New Testament." They reply, "Oh, you belong to the church of the New Testament? I never heard of that one."

Isn't that the way we think today? In terms of organizational affiliation instead of Christ affiliation?

H. G. Wells in his *Outline of History* said in 1920, "It is necessary that we should recall the reader's attention to the profound differences between this fully developed Christianity [of the fourth century] and the teaching of Jesus of Nazareth....It was not priestly, it had no consecrated temple, and no altar. It had no rites and ceremonies. Its sacrifice was 'a broken and a contrite heart.' Its only organization was an organization of preachers, and its chief function was the sermon.

"....though it preserved as its nucleus the teachings of Jesus in the Gospels, was mainly a priestly religion....the centre of its elaborate ritual was an altar...And it had a rapidly developing organization of deacons, priests, and bishops." [2]

Jesus prayed over and over that we may be one (John 17). He wouldn't have prayed for the impossible.

Perfect Pattern, Imperfect People

The basis of Christian unity is found in John 17:11 where Jesus said [caps mine], "Holy Father, protect them by the power of YOUR NAME – the NAME YOU GAVE ME – so that THEY MAY BE ONE as we are one."

Whose name do we carry? Are we hyphenated Christians? Do we call ourselves Baptist-Christians, Lutheran-Christians, Presbyterian-Christians, Nazarene-Christians, Mennonite-Christians?

A divided church cannot win the world to Christ. As long as we delay winning the world to Christ as Jesus commanded just before he re-entered heaven, we delay his return.

The president of a denominational theological seminary long ago said in an address, "Denominationalism is dead at the roots, but not yet in the branches. In time, the branches will wither and denominationalism will be dead....there is no excuse now for divisions." [3]

Martin Luther said, "I pray you to leave my name alone, and call not yourselves Lutherans, but Christians. Who is Luther? My doctrine is not mine! I have not been crucified for anyone. St. Paul (1 Cor. chapters one and three) would not have that any should call themselves of Paul, nor of Peter, but of Christ. How, then, does it benefit me, a miserable bag of dust and ashes, to give my name to the children of Christ? Cease, my dear friends, to cling to these party names and distinctions; away with them all; and let us call ourselves only Christians after him from whom our doctrine comes." [4]

John Wesley said in the preface of his *Notes on the New Testament*, "Would to God that all party names, and unscriptural phrases and forms, which have divided the Christian world, were forgot; and that we might agree to sit down together as humble loving disciples, at the feet of our common Master, to hear His word, to imbibe His Spirit, and to transcribe His life into our own." [5]

Jesus emphasized our oneness again just before he left the earth in Matthew 28:19. "Therefore go, and make disciples of all nations, baptizing them in the name of the Father and of the Son and of the Holy Spirit." What is that name?

Philippians 2:9-11 says, "Therefore God exalted him to the highest place and gave him the name that is above every name, that at the name of Jesus every knee should bow, in heaven and on earth and under the earth, and every tongue confess that Jesus Christ is Lord, to the glory of God the Father."

Well, what about our creed books—the books that explain what we must do be accepted by a particular denomination? Do we actually believe we can clarify God's Word? Do we actually believe God is not capable of writing something we can all believe in alike?

Have you ever read your denomination's creed? It may surprise you. Most creeds cover a few general beliefs that most everyone agrees with, but then it speaks to a particular belief that separates that religious body from others. Examine several creeds for yourself. You will find that they are divisive, for they emphasize mostly matters of opinion. Honest opinion, but still opinion.

H. G. Wells said regarding religion in Europe, "Its priests and bishops were more and more men molded to creeds and dogmas and set procedures; by the time they became cardinals or popes they were usually oldish men, habituated to a political struggle for immediate ends and no longer capable of worldwide views. They no longer wanted to see the Kingdom of God established in the hearts of men—they had forgotten about that; they wanted to see the power of the church, which was their own power, dominating men....

"They were intolerant of questions or dissent, not because they were sure of their faith, but because they were not. They wanted conformity for reasons of policy....This was a spirit entirely counter to that of Jesus of Nazareth. We do not hear of his smacking the faces or wringing the wrists of recalcitrant or unresponsive disciples." [6]

If a creed is more than the Bible, it is too much. If it is less than the Bible, it is too little. If it is the same as the Bible, why do we need it? Instead of swearing on our creed books, instead of signing oaths that we agree with our creed books, why don't we swear on the Bible and sign oaths that we agree with the Bible?

Oh, blessed Jesus. Forgive our arrogance.

Institutionalizing the Church

Years ago a parable went around something like this. A demon needed advice from a devil on how to discourage the church in his area because someone had gotten hold of a grain of truth. If used properly, it could blow up the devil's whole business.

The demon was advised by the devil, "Just tempt him to take that grain of truth and organize it. Make it the basis of some kind of society, or lodge, or club. Then he'll spend his time running the club, and he won't have any time to use the truth against us."

The last anyone heard, the grain of truth, which was the nucleus of the organization he founded, was left useless in a glass case in the lobby of the building that the new organization erected.

The Pharisees in Jesus' day were institutionalists. They had added all kinds of traditions to the Law of Moses. They had added hundreds of rules to explain what people must do to keep each of Moses' laws.

In the four-volume *Code of Jewish Law* put out by the Hebrew Publishing Company, there are listed twenty-one explicit rules governing the rite of hand washing before eating. Here are just some of them:

If the food eaten is smaller than an egg, I must wash my hands but I do not have to say the benediction. No part of my hand up to the wrist must be untouched, including my fingertips and between each finger. I must first clean my fingernails so there is no obstruction between the water and my fingers. Just in case I accidentally miss a spot, I should do it twice. Further, as I wet my hands, they must be palm up in accordance with Psalm 134:2 ("lift up your hands"). If my unclean hand touches my clean one, I must start over. [7]

We may think this is ridiculous. But is it any more ridiculous than the volumes each denomination has written to explain the details of how we must follow a particular command of Jesus?

Jesus said in Mark 7:6-9, "'These people honor me with their lips, but their hearts are far from me. They worship me in vain; their teachings are but rules taught by men.' You have let go of the commands of God and are holding on to the traditions of men."

The Jews needed to go back. Back before all the volumes of traditional laws had muddied the simplicity of God's Law given to Moses 2000 years before. They needed to let go. Can we let go of our creeds and denominationalism? Is it possible? Are our egos too relentlessly strong?

What would happen if Jesus visited today and told us the same things he told the Jews? Would Jesus view all those modern church laws a help? Or a hindrance? Could we go back? Back before all the volumes of church laws that muddy up the simplicity of God's Law and divide us from each other?

Do we have the courage to do what the Jewish leaders could not bring themselves to do?

The Pharisees were institutionalists, just as denominationalists are today. Jesus was an idealist, and short on organization. Did Jesus make a mistake? Jesus disregarded the Pharisees' human authority and all their laws. So they murdered him rather than let go.

The only organization set up for the church was to have elders/bishops (same office) and deacons in every church (congregation) as explained in 1st Timothy 3 and Titus 1. These Scriptures give qualifications, so we know they were official positions in the church. Nothing was ever said about one elder/bishop being over the others within the congregation, or one being over other congregations. Nor was any arrangement made for a meeting of delegates to vote on beliefs.

Actually, it was not until about the time of the apostle John's death around 95 AD that several congregations appointed one elder to be head over the other elders and be called a bishop. In 120 AD the bishop of the largest congregation in some metropolitan areas told the other congregations he was head over them. A century later these bishops were being called papa/pope/father/patriarch. In 300 AD, the bishops of the strongest cities in a province announced they were archbishops. In 700 AD the strongest bishop among all the provinces in the known world announced he was head over all the others. He was called the pope.

One seemingly innocent decision was not so innocent after all. God's command had been tampered with. The world reeled from it for centuries to come.

As far as Councils go, it is great for Christians to get together and talk about their belief in the Bible and to reaffirm each other. But it is going beyond the scope of the Bible for representatives of congregations to come together as delegates to do our thinking for us and vote on what we must believe.

There was only one Council mentioned in the Bible and it was made up of "the apostles and elders" (Acts 15:2 and 6) who "met to consider....." Since we have no apostles today, all that is left are elders. Elders are to have authority over their own congregation as its local Council.

1st Samuel 10:10-19 tells of the Israelites insisting on having an earthly king. God said they had rejected him from being their king. So, too, today we have appointed head pastors/shepherds and rejected Jesus from being our head Shepherd. They wanted a king they could see, not one they could not see. Today, we want a shepherd we can see, not one we cannot see. So we have our denominational bishops and presidents.

Oh, Jesus. Forgive us for trying to improve on you.

Side-Tracking our Purpose

"I Am Quitting My church to Preach" appeared in *Sunset Magazine* years ago. In it James L. Gordon wrote, "I find myself more interested in ideas than in institutions. An idea always loses force as it becomes institutionalized. The modern preacher is under pressure to show results in membership and money. He is expected to build up the church. The idea of building up humanity is always a secondary consideration. To organize a strong social circle is more to the mind of the churchman than large congregations or inspirational services....

"So I want a pulpit unhampered by the machinery of modern ecclesiasticism. I believe in organization but I also know that when truth is organized and institutionalized, it loses something of its original force and vitality." [8]

Many who have gone into the ministry have come back out of it disillusioned with the politics. Basically all of them enter the ministry to serve and save the lost. But they get caught up in having to answer to the larger organization. He has to fall in line or jeopardize his job.

Organization leads to spiritual pride. Organization leads to people lording it over the flock. Organization leads to accusations of being "non-cooperative." Organization leads to discharging ministers of the Word because they do not compete well enough with the organization down the street. Organization leads to critical fire by newspapers, true seekers, and atheists. Organization leads to scrambling for place and position.

In 1925, a grand effort was made to unite several denominations. They included the Methodists, some Congregationalists, and part of the Presbyterians. But they ended up with another denomination. Although they called themselves the United church, they immediately formed a hierarchy and headquarters. They'd gone right back to what they'd separated from. Why? Because of over-organization. Do people not feel they are religious unless they are organized?

We have become organization crazy. We think organization is power. We end up talking about "our" denomination, "our" world interests, "our church." We have made a test of fellowship out of "our" church. The only kind of power it engenders is individual power, and distraction from the power of Jesus and his gospel.

When organization grew, its only logical outcome was a human head and headquarters, the papacy. What became of the Holy Spirit? The institutionalized church is the greatest enemy of true Christianity today. We have come to trust the organization instead of Jesus Christ and his Word alone.

Organization results in jealousies, power plays, politics, wrath, strife, contention. True, a great organization carries great prestige. Does not such prestige come at the expense of the prestige of Jesus Christ?

H. G. Wells said in his history of Europe, "The idea of stamping out all controversy and division, stamping out all thought, by imposing one dogmatic creed upon all believers, is an altogether autocratic idea, it is the idea of the single-handed man who feels that to work at all he must be free from opposition and criticism.

"The history of the church under [Emperor Constantine's] influence now becomes, therefore, a history of the violent struggles that were bound to follow....From him the church acquired the disposition to be authoritative and unquestioned, to develop a centralized organization and run parallel to the empire." [9]

Indeed, today, some denominational hierarchies have developed into an empire. The work of the living Christ does not depend on any human organization.

The greatest advances in Christianity are made on the local level with local decisions. But often local outreach programs go unled because our leaders are busy with the greater organization, the denominational headquarters. The Organization Spirit is crowding out the Holy Spirit.

Jesus said, "All authority in heaven and on earth has been given to me" (Matthew 28:18). Not a head organization at some headquarters somewhere. Not a head president or bishop or pope somewhere. The only head over the local congregation is Jesus.

Some time ago, Episcopal church members including the chairman of the national commission on evangelism and several bishops wrote this letter to their headquarters:

"The church today is incomparably rich in money, organization, influence, power, and yet it failed to produce anything like apostolic results. For example, our communion, with its 135 bishops, more than 5000 priests and more than a million communicants, obtained a net gain last year of only 25,000 members, which means that with all our resources it took 50 persons to add one communicant."[10]

That was nearly a century ago. What would the figures be like today? Dare we say today it takes at least 200 people to save one soul? Are we neglecting the salvation of souls so we may build up the organization?

Several years ago, a group of major denominations ministers published this plea:

"The Men's church League is alarmed because one-third of all the Presbyterian, Northern Baptists and Methodist Episcopal churches had no converts last year — a total of 11,394 churches...J. Earle Edwards, a Baptist preacher, is reported to have said that the trouble is due to red tape, sectarian organization, theology, jealousy - in fact, to everything but Jesus Christ and His spirit.

"We recommend the abolition of sectarian organization, both in its competitive and monopolistic phases, and the return to the simple church of Christ according to the New Testament pattern; we recommend the cutting away of red tape and cumbersome machinery in order that there may be breathing room for the spirit and free use of initiative in going about the Father's business." [11]

When the church of the first century was solely congregational with its only ultimate head above the elders being Jesus Christ, it was unconquerable. Rivers of early Christians' blood fertilized the fields white unto harvest with the seed, the Word of God.

Blessed Jesus, we have forgotten how lost we were in our sins, and we have forgotten the lost around us. Please forgive us.

Prejudice

Everyone agrees that denominationalism is not preferred over unity. James 2:9 says we are not to have respect of persons, and yet we do this with our denominationalism. If division in the body of Christ is good, we should follow it to its logical conclusion and encourage each person to build a religion unto self and never assemble with others.

Paul told the church at Corinth with all their divisiveness that they were carnal; that is, worldly (1st Corinthians 1:10-13; 3:3-4). Philippians 2:1-5 says we are to be "one in spirit and purpose. Do nothing out of selfish ambition or vain conceit, but in humility consider others better than yourselves. Each of you should look not only to your own interests, but also to the interests of others."

The apostle Peter said we were to be all likeminded (1st Peter 3:8). The brother of Jesus said we who murmur, complain and walk after our lusts show respect of persons for the sake of gaining the advantage (Jude 16).

Galatians 5:19-21 lists 15 sins including sexual immorality and witchcraft; yet over half refer to divisiveness: Hatred, discord, jealousy, fits of rage (temper tantrums), selfish ambition, dissensions, factions, envy.

James, a brother of Jesus, warned in 3:14-16, "But if you

harbor bitter envy and selfish ambition in your hearts, do not boast about it or deny the truth. such 'wisdom' does not come down from heaven but is earthly, unspiritual, of the devil."

The great reformers who broke away from the Catholic church had the right idea and were certainly blessed. But they did not go far enough. They eliminated things they disliked about the Catholic church, and then kept what they did like.

Luther eliminated paying indulgences and having a separate priesthood, believing in the priesthood of all believers saved by grace. That was good. Calvin eliminated approval of the church for one's salvation, believing it to be a personal experience. That was good. Wesley eliminated formalism in favor of methodism. That was good. Knox eliminated papism in favor of presbyterianism. That was good. But none went all the way back. That was not good.

John Godfrey Saxe explained eloquently what each great Reformer accomplished [2]:

It was six men of Hindustan, to learning much inclined,
Who went to see the elephant, (Though all of them were blind)
That each by observation might satisfy his mind.

The first approached the elephant, and happening to fall
Against his broad and sturdy side, at once began to bawl,
"God bless me! but the elephant is very much like a wall!"

The second feeling of the tusk cried, "Ho, What have we here
So very round and smooth and sharp? to me 'tis very clear
This wonder of an elephant is very like a spear.

The third approached the animals, and happening to take
The squirming trunk within his hands, thus boldly up he spake:
"I see," quoth he, "the elephant is very like a snake."

The fourth reached out his eager hand, and felt about the knee,
"What most this wondrous beast is like is mighty plain," quoth he;
" 'Tis clear enough the elephant is very like a tree."

Fifth who chanced to touch the ear, said, "E'en the blindest man
Can tell what this resembles most; deny the fact who can.
This marvel of an elephant is very like a fan."

> *The sixth no sooner had begun about the beast to grope,*
> *Then seizing on the swinging tail, that fell within his scope,*
> *"I see," quoth he, "the elephant is very like a rope."*
>
> *And so these men of Hindustan disputed loud and long,*
> *Each in his own opinion exceeding stiff and strong,*
> *Though each was partly in the right, and all were in the wrong.*
>
> *So often in theologic wars the disputants, I ween,*
> *Rail on in utter ignorance of what each other mean*
> *And prate about an elephant not one of them has seen!*

May the religious leaders of our land fall to their knees, ask God's forgiveness, then rise to resign from denominational positions in councils, synods and headquarters, and influence their congregations to function as independent bodies led only by the New Testament.

Blessed Savior. You looked at us in our sinfulness and saw some good in us — enough that was worth saving. How unworthy we still are. But we're trying. Help us try harder.

Making Decisions for Us

Indeed, it seems a fairly reliable guess that 90% of all people have no theological idea why they belong to the denomination they do. So why do they allow such division?

We allow it because regular people do not study the Word of God for themselves. We - in our laziness - are willing to take the word of ministers who may or may not be defending their standing in their denominational organization. And we allow it because we have closed minds to protect our egos. We refuse to believe we may believe different from the Bible.

I shared the gospel message with one woman for nearly two years. She was dying. She admitted that where she went to church (a large and powerful denomination) it had always been just a social club with the preacher preaching philosophy. She didn't even know there was an Old and New Testament in the Bible. When I shared the gospel message with her right out of the Bible, she was almost persuaded until she consulted with her preacher. He said she didn't have to do any of that. She reasoned that, since he had a degree in religion, he must be right. She went to her grave believing in this man who will himself be judged by God based on the very Bible he denied to her.

In *The Dilemmas of Jesus* James Black, Minister of the United Free Church in Edinburgh, Scotland, is reported in the book *Be One*, as having said this:

"So many of us do not trust Jesus for Himself, but we trust in what lesser authorities say about Him....We are cursed with experts and authorities. It may be a church, or a book, or a creed, or a man - what does it matter? It is always the same irreligious thing. 'Authority' is always irreligious!

"....we quote an article in a creed....This is what the creed says, you poor mouse! ...Or, we quote a church. Here is the authority of the saints and fathers, the decrees of the church....Surely you do not set your little mind up against that!

"....It is sheer mental ruin, especially in religion. 'What think ye of Jesus?' - and you for yourself are as able to settle your personal relation to Him as any scholar that was ever born. Jesus believed that the simplest soul could accept Him as fully as Lord and Master, and could do it, - nay, must do it - out of his own heart and mind. Jesus is His own and only authority." [13]

Jesus never died to build any organization. He died to save individuals who, as a result, gather together in a simply-organized commune of believers for encouragement.

H. G. Wells said, "It is difficult to read the surviving literature of the time without a strong sense of the dogmatism, the spites, rivalries, and pedantries of the men who tore Christianity to pieces for the sake of these theological refinements." [14]

Oh, blessed Jesus. Forgive us.

Married to Our Institution

There have been two groups of people within the church who have been most critical of our institutionalism. The first have been those that organized religion often identified as "splinter groups," "off-shoots," or even "heretics." The real intention of these groups are covered in the last chapter of this book.

The other group that has criticized our institutionalism are missionaries in foreign countries, isolated from most any kind of believer in Christ. Most denominations would be surprised to know that the missionaries they sent out actually hob-nobbed with missionaries of other denominations, all of whom left behind the confusion of their individual creeds and learned to rely only on the simple New Testament.

What breaks down their artificial boundaries? Their loneliness, craving for other Christian companionship, and their longing to save souls. These missionaries refuse to get involved in dogmatic disputes because all they want to do is convert the lost. Thoughts of opinionated dogma leave their mind completely for more important business, and they do not teach their denomination's dogma to new converts.

Furthermore, denominational headquarters would be surprised to know that these missionaries are converting people, giving them the Bible, then staying out of their way while the local people launch out to convert still others.

Instead, denominational headquarters tell its members they must maintain their particular standard of dogmas at all costs. They cannot tolerate untrained and uncontrolled new converts to propagate the gospel.

Their attitude of "cannot allow" and "cannot tolerate" is obviously the attitude of a superior, a supervisor, one who sets himself up as a parent, a father, a papa, a pope. The institutionalized church hierarchy has laid claim of lordship over our faith - The Faith - unwilling to relinquish it to Jesus.

Several years ago, missionary Roland Allen wrote *The Spontaneous Expansion of the church* for missionaries, but which has applications for every congregation. In the chapter on "Fear for the Doctrine" note what Allen says:

"On what then do we rely for the exercise of this authority? Without doubt we rely upon our prestige....When we say we must maintain our standard, we certainly mean that it is our standard and not their standard [or the Lord's]....

"....a standard of doctrine...maintained by an external authority as a code of laws can be enforced by a conquering government upon a subject people. How do we attempt to maintain it? First we make the preparation for baptism long and difficult by insisting upon each convert learning what is for very many of them difficult verbal lessons [from our creeds]. Multitudes of our converts are totally unfamiliar with the kind of abstract language....

"We train the teachers...in schools and theological colleges, so that they can understand our use of abstract terms and can learn at least verbally our doctrinal expressions....From amongst these teachers we select the men who repeat best...our point of view...then ordain them with great confidence that they will teach nothing but what they have learned from us. And these men we put into positions of greater authority....

"The results...(1) Terrible sterility....We have taught them to depend upon us, rather than upon Christ....(2) The Doctrine has been maintained by external authority, but it has hampered the thought of the people...begin to feel this dimly and to resent it." [15]

From whence do the great heresies of the church arise? Not from people out in the trenches trying to reach, teach, and convert people to Christ for their soul's salvation. Not from the unordained, the officially unrecognized does it come. Heresies arise from the educated and philosophical who would boast of their superior minds and superior grasp of things holy and religious.

In his chapter on organization Allen says: "There is a horrible tendency for an organization to grow in importance till it overshadows the end of its existence, and begins to exist for itself....Our love of organization leads us to rely upon it....

"Indeed, we modernists are mesmerized with organization.

We pride ourselves in our developmental and administrative skills. But when it comes to spreading the Gospel, our love for organization drowns us. For we are too preoccupied with material things. As a result, we ultimately try to organize spiritual forces.

"Our organization immobilizes," Allen goes on. "Great opportunities, widespread movements towards Christ, must be neglected rather than that these institutions should lack workers...The whole system of societies, boards, offices, accounts, contracts with [pastors], statistical returns, reports reeks of it." [16]

When church Councils were instituted, the fundamental simplicities of proclaiming the gospel to the lost became slighted.

Can we comprehend Paul being solemnly appointed archbishop of Europe? How about Philip serving as parish priest of Macedonia? Or perhaps Luke traveling up and down Italy to administer the sacraments? Imagine the seven churches of Asia Minor being denied the sacraments because the Apostle John is sidetracked on the Isle Patmos. Envision Peter sending urgent appeals to Jerusalem for a priest for Ephesus, or a bishop for Spain. None of this is even hinted at in the Bible. Yet we dare to try to improve on the Bible.

Can you imagine new converts being told there is a distant church government out there to which they could vote to send a representative to discuss something which they do not understand. Can you conceive new converts being informed an ecclesiastic body exists somewhere out there on which they must rely for their beliefs? Somewhere out there in church hierarchy "heaven?"

In his chapter on "Ecclesiastical Organization" Allen says:

"Like Nebuchadnezzar's image, [the church's] head was of gold, its belly of brass, and its feet part of iron and part of clay. It stood upon feet of iron and clay, paid lay workers, and congregations which were not churches; its head was high uplifted, one solitary potentate, the bishop; and between these there was an utterly inadequate number of [clergy], quite unable to provide nourishment for the whole; but strong and exclusive as brass." [17]

Spontaneous expansion of a congregation and of the church

of Christ must be free; it cannot be under an outsider's control, whether ours or someone else's.

The New Testament never went into an anxious appeal for Christians to go out and spread the gospel. Irregardless, the church spread like wildfire in the first century, and following their ways can create the same thing for us 21 centuries later.

Spontaneous growth means creating an irresistible atmosphere to which people are drawn so they, too, may discover the secret of life. Spontaneous growth means members telling others of Jesus' love for them as expressed through the Bible itself and loving acts of other Christians. Spontaneous growth also means so many members added that other congregations are started, then left to themselves to begin the divine cycle anew.

Allen explains, "I know not how it may appear to others, but to me this unexhorted, unorganized, spontaneous expansion has a charm far beyond that of our modern highly organized [denominations]. I delight to think that a Christian traveling on his business could preach Christ....

"I suspect...I am not alone in this strange preference, and that many others read their Bibles and find there with relief a welcome escape from our material appeals for funds and our methods of moving heaven and earth to make a proselyte.

"But men say that such relief can only be for dreamers....I must...admit that...it is true...if it is really better that paid [clergy] be sent out by an elaborately organized office, and be supported by a department, and directed by a headquarters staff; if it is really true that our elaborate machinery is a great improvement on ancient practice; and that to carry the knowledge of Christ throughout the world it is in fact more efficient than the simpler methods of the apostolic age....

"But if we [ministers], toiling under the burden of our organizations, sigh for that spontaneous freedom of expanding life, it is because we see in it something divine, something in its very nature profoundly efficient, something which we would gladly recover, something which the elaboration of our modern machinery obscures and deadens and kills." [18]

What is it that causes the church to grow spontaneously? It's in the power of the secret. There is something exciting and wonderful and magical in sharing a secret. The hearer is flattered at the trust shown. After all, a secret could be betrayed. What is the secret?

"I did some terrible things. I was going to be punished for them, but this stranger came along and offered to take my punishment for me."

"What stranger?"

"Jesus."

The human spirit automatically wants to share such a marvelous secret, but the Christian spirit wants more. The Christian spirit wants to spread the good news that this Jesus will take their place for their punishment too. Then all those new Christians in turn want to spread the word.

Such a person cannot relieve his own mind until he has told it and told it and told it. And yet, the institutionalized church says, "Now wait a minute. You're too new of a Christian. You need to be grounded in the faith."

So the leaders ground them in the faith so far, that they never get up, as Jack Exum used to say. Why do Christian leaders run from it? Allen explains that it is because of their need to control.

"We fear it because we feel that it is something that we cannot control....'The wind bloweth where it listeth,' said Christ, and spontaneous activity is a movement of the Spirit in the individual and in the church, and we cannot control the Spirit....For if we cannot control it, it is because it is too great, not because it is too small for us. The great things of God are beyond our control....

"There is always something terrifying in the feeling that we are letting loose a force which we cannot control ....Whether we consider our doctrine, or our civilization, or our morals, or our organization, in relation to a spontaneous expansion of the church, we are seized with terror, terror lest spontaneous expansion should lead to disorder." [19]

Allen goes on to explain the disastrous results in the trenches of life among lost souls.

"Spontaneous expansion begins with individual expression,

it proceeds to corporate expression, and if the corporate expression is checked there is again a danger of disorder. The denial of...self-government, seems at the moment to be a great security for order...it represses the instinct for self-propagation....

"The momentary security is thus gained at a serious cost....The instinct for expression is so strong that it cannot long be restrained. Then must be repeated...the struggle...Here, too, it is not the desire for expression which produces the disorder, it is the desire breaking out against order because it cannot express itself within the order which it knows. That, too, is grievous; it means the rending of the body; and that is a sore evil and a source of evil to the whole body." [20]

When the church first multiplied, Satan tried to induce the apostles to control the new Gentile Christians by binding much of the Law of Moses on them. The apostles resisted and refused to fall into the control trap.

This is Satan's greatest weapon in the church. If he can build a hedge of creeds and regulations around an organization, it can choke out the primary purpose of the church's existence, and in the process choke out the church.

A century ago in Africa, there was discovered a simple New Testament church of some 100 Christians. One of the village members had obtained a New Testament and learned to read it. He taught his own friends and the good news spread. They even built a little church building. They met every morning before going to work on their farms and after they got home in the evening to learn more about what was in this New Testament.

Some years later in Tauran, Borneo, a congregation was discovered of over 40 Christians. They had come from China. One of their number had been converted to Christianity back in China. He taught them what he knew and they built a little church building. They came in contact with no other Christians for ten years; all they had was the New Testament.

The spontaneous expansion of the church requires no elaborate organization, no large finances, no great numbers of clergy and paid laity. It begins with the work of one person sharing the secret.

Allen concludes thusly: "The missionaries who spread the Gospel and established the church throughout the lands round the Mediterranean are not known to us as men of great learning or ability. Most of them are not known by name at all....What is needed is the kind of faith which, uniting a man to Christ, sets him on fire. Such a man can believe that others finding Christ will be set on fire also." [21]

Oh, God. This is such a new concept I am learning. We thought all this organizing was for the betterment of the church. Could we have been wrong?

Power of the Individual

The American Bible Society has reported instances of people coming to simple first-century Christianity with just the use of their Bible back in the late 1800s and early 1900s when missionary work was at its height. The book *Be One* gives this account:

"When a Chinese man was visiting several hundred miles away from home, a missionary gave him a New Testament. He knew nothing of Christianity, but he read the Book. He became interested in the Christ and called in his friends and neighbors and read to them. They came to believe that Jesus is the Son of God, and that salvation from all sin is to be found through Him.

"They repented of their evil lives, and seeing in the Book where penitent believers were baptized, the man had someone bury him in baptism, and he baptized the other believers. They elected such officers as they read of in the New Testament....

"Of what denomination were they? They were not Catholic. They had never heard of the pope, and certainly did not acknowledge his authority in any slightest particular. They were not protestants. They had nothing against which to protest." [22]

Through the centuries the church of the New Testament has survived in remote corners away from the bombardment of the institutional church. Just look up some of these movements. Outsiders named them after their leader, though they wanted to just be called Christians. Encyclopedias of general knowledge and encyclopedias of religion often call these groups "heretics" because they did not fall in line with "organized religion."

But that did not stop them. They continued to grow. They grew like wildfire. Their leaders went around to the denominations asking people to put away their denominational allegiance and align themselves only with Jesus Christ and him crucified. These groups are represented in the last chapter.

They exist even today. They are everywhere. We do not always know about them because they are not represented by a world headquarters. But Jesus knows who they are, because he has them registered in his headquarters, heaven.

The church began and thrived with individuals. It can do so again.

The truly great work of the church has always been accomplished with the least amount of organization. The apostles and their unorganized friends created the church. Paul was not accountable to a great organization; he only reported in to his home congregation who had encouraged him to go out and preach.

After freedom of religion became more predominant, with governments not dictating which church their citizens must belonged to, more and more denominations arose with their own organization at some world headquarters somewhere. But David Livingstone, the most famous missionary to Africa, refused to come under the supervision of any organization or other restorationists of first-century Christianity around the world followed the Word of God so exclusively that the organized religions of their day withdrew from them.

Great restorationists, people who believe in restoring the church of the first century, call themselves out of denominationalism and separate themselves from the power of the political machinery that runs them all.

Great restorationists—the mechanics, the computer operators, the financial analysts, the waiters, the salespeople, the engineers, the cab drivers, the daycare workers, the contractors—all the great restorationists call themselves out of denominationalism, out of institutionalism, and into the light of simple New Testament Christianity.

Barton W. Stone and his congregation drew up a **last will and testament** of their presbytery in Kentucky nearly two centuries ago. This is how it read:

"We will that this body die, be dissolved, and sink into union with the body of Christ at large; for there is but one body and one Spirit, even as we are called in one hope of our calling....We will that our power of making laws for the government of the church and executing them by delegated authority forever cease; that the people may have free course to the Bible, and adopt the law of the spirit of life in Christ Jesus." [23]

But God, this requires so much courage. What if I cannot find anyone else who agrees with me? Help me.

That They May Be One

The Christian world is so divided, we exist in a trap, trying to win people to the institutionalized church instead of to Jesus Christ. Our institutionalization has become the source of our power instead of the Spirit-breathed gospel of salvation.

The other cause of our divisiveness is our arguments over things that are either unprovable (when Christ will return) or issues which the Scriptures show different points of view that we have not yet learned to balance (we were predestined, but still have free will). Amazing as it may seem, none of us is perfect in understanding. Now all that is left is for us to admit it. Can we? Every one of us?

Sometimes, when congregations go through change, they go through "holy wars." Most any change will create the loss of some members who decide to go to church where they still do things the old way. That is their right. They are just not ready yet to give up prided opinions. They are just not ready to give up the traditional and predictable yet. Let us not allow them to discourage us. Let us be their example.

There is so much more that we in the Christian world can unite on. There is so much more that everyone in Christendom agrees with. It is the simple parts of the scripture. So simple. So dynamic. Things that we all agree on.

1. EVERYONE AGREES the name "Christian" is scriptural.

2. EVERYONE AGREES that we must hear the gospel that Jesus died in our place with our sins on the cross, then conquered death three days later.

3. EVERYONE AGREES that we must believe it to be saved.

4. EVERYONE AGREES we must be willing to tell others that we believe it.

5. EVERYONE AGREES we must ask God to forgive us for our sins.

6. EVERYONE AGREES that baptism is in the Bible, Jesus himself was baptized, and he commanded it of others.

7. EVERYONE AGREES we must sing and pray and read the Bible.

8. EVERYONE AGREES we must partake of the Lord's Supper.

And there it is. The basics of Christianity. Actually, when we stop to think about it, we agree on many more things than we disagree on. As the song from World War II days said, why not eliminate the negative? Why not accentuate the positive?

The apostle Paul wrote a strong letter to the church in Corinth for their spiritual immaturity and carnality. Shortly after, he sent them another letter. In it he said, "'Therefore come out from them and be separate,' says the Lord" (6:17).

Do we dare make Jesus Christ the only head outside of our congregation, and heaven our only headquarters? Do we have the courage? Previous chapters in this book told how church institutionalism built up through the centuries, and about those who dared stand up against it.

The record of their tortures and deaths by the thousands stands as a vivid testimony to people's determination to be Christians only, and to simply belong to the church headquartered only in heaven. They believed it was worth dying for. Do we believe it is worth living for?

Neither Catholic, Protestant, Nor Jew

While we're arguing and nitpicking and tearing each other down, more and more people are growing more and more lonely. While we're spatting and ripping each other apart, more and more people are dying in their sins. In all our arguing, perhaps we, too, have been left alone by Jesus. Alone, and we don't even know it.

Division is a sin. Leave it behind. Let us all begin with a blank sheet of paper. Let each member read through the Bible and list as s/he goes what is commanded for Christians to do, and refuse to go beyond it. Throw the rest away. Throw away all creeds. Disband all organizations outside the congregation. Decry all names but the name of Jesus Christ.

Division is a sin. Would to God we could unite and call ourselves simply Christians, and identify the place where we meet simply as "the church on _____ street in _____ town."

If an entire congregation decides to do so, they can sign a document deeding their property to the newly formed non-denominational congregation. Or they may decide not to even have a building if such is a stumbling block in their community, and meet in a school or civic auditorium instead.

In the book *Be One* by Norris Jacob Reasner, he suggests that congregations affiliated with national and world denominations draw up a document dissolving itself into union with the church of Christ headquartered only in heaven.

"WHEREAS it is the supreme purpose of this church to exalt Christ in all things, by complete surrender to His will, that 'In all things He may have the pre-eminence;'

"AND WHEREAS He prayed for believers upon Him, of all ages of the world's history, 'That they may all be one;' [24]

"AND WHEREAS there are _____ [state the number] of organized churches in this community, where He would have but one body of believers;

"NOW THEREFORE be it resolved by the _____ church in regular, congregation assembled, that we stand ready to dissolve our organization, and as individuals, unite with the individuals of any and each church that will take like action, to form a new congregation of believers upon Christ,

"The said new congregation agreeing to recognize no authority between that of the local congregation and the Lord Jesus Christ, but recognizing His unlimited authority in all things.

"The new church so formed is to take the New Testament as its sole written authority, and before permitting, requiring, or prohibiting any practice as a Christian practice of the congregation, to find where it was authorized by commandment, or approved in the practice of, or prohibited by, inspired men as recorded in the New Testament.

"The new church is to have no official affiliation with any other organization, but all individuals are to be asked to designate the agency they desire to have handle their every offerings for 'others.'

"It is also understood that no minister shall be employed by the new church organization who does not heartily endorse to these sentiments." [25]

There may be individuals reading this book with no denominational affiliation or no support for complete restoration from within their congregation. Individuals wishing to unite with others who wish to be just New Testament Christians—no more and no less—may not know where to find others with this same desire.

Place a sizeable ad in the newspaper. It may take a year to save enough to pay for an ad large enough to attract attention. But do it. There are others out there searching for you, just as you are searching for them.

Contact ministers in your community. Ask them if they desire non-denominationalism. If so, spend time with them. Ask them to talk to their congregations to see if others feel the same way.

Do not give a name to the new congregation other than "the church." Do not identify yourself as anything other than "Christians." If people try to pigeon hole you, tell them in no uncertain terms that you reject any name they may call you other than Christ's name.

But beware! Once out, we must be careful not to develop another denomination.

Two hundred years ago when a great restoration movement

occurred in the U.S., these ministers went from city to city preaching in every denomination they could find—Presbyterian, Baptist, Methodist, Unitarian, Episcopal. These men preached unity in all kinds of denominations, and did so unless they were told not to come back. But never did these restorationists turn them away. All they had to do is abide by one rule: Where the Bible speaks, we speak. Where the Bible is silent, be silent.

In India, seminars are being held all over the country wherein denominational preachers are taught simple New Testament Christianity. As a result, they are returning to their congregations and becoming autonomous with no creed but the Bible. The first to come over to the new movement in many of these places were and are the clergy who knew first-hand the evils of organization beyond the congregational level.

Let go of all these burdens. They are wasting our energy. Let us from now on determine to concentrate only on our own congregation and our own neighborhood and our own sphere of influence. Let us from now on determine to concentrate on ways to show God's love to a lost and wandering world. Then we won't have time for the opinions. Opinions must be lost in the sea of oblivion. Floating atop that sea is a ship of victory.

Jesus is there in that ship. He is the captain. He cries out to all of us, "PEACE! BE STILL!" Can we allow the storms within our souls to have peace? Can we allow the storms within our souls to be still? Only then can we show the lost how to have peace and how to "be still and know that I am God" (Psalm 46:10) of their lives now and forever.

Tears will flow. Tears of sadness and tears of joy. Sadness for all the divisiveness that has separated us for so very long. Joy for those with which we unite for the express purpose of leading the world to Christ.

Is "coming out from among them" easy? Absolutely not. It is not as difficult for people who have given up going to church altogether out of frustration. But for congregations breaking away from a denomination, or individuals breaking away from institutionalized churches, it could be the hardest thing you ever did.

Well-meaning friends who either do not want you to make them look bad, or who have not read enough Scriptures to understand what you are doing, will pressure you to return. You will be gossiped about, receive phone calls of friends who will thereafter be afraid to be seen associating with you, receive letters of warning, perhaps be disfellowshipped from the congregation you are leaving, and maybe even written up in some kind of church paper.

On the other hand, look at what the paid "clergy" would go through to dissolve their denomination. They would be voting themselves out of a job. Some can do it, as is shown below, but most cannot without our support.

Just look at the ecumenical movement. In 1910 the first World Missionary Conference in Scotland met because missionaries did not want to explain denominational differences to converts in other countries. But it was never considered an official conference by the denominations.

In 1921 the International Missionary Council met, but all it accomplished was to form more Councils in Asia and Africa.

In 1924 the Conference on Politics, Economics and Citizenship met in England, but it had nothing to do with doctrinal differences. In 1925, the Universal Conference on Life and Work met in Sweden, but it was similar.

In 1927 the World Conference on Faith and Order met, but all they accomplished was help each other understand their denomination's unique beliefs better.

Finally in 1948, the World Council of Churches was formed, combining the Faith and Order and the Politics and Economics Councils, and in 1961 it absorbed the International Missionary Council. But the paid hierarchy of each church maintains its paid position. No one is going to vote their denomination out of existence and in the process vote themselves out of a job.

Years ago when Lee Iacocca took over Chrysler to save it from bankruptcy, he gave orders to all division heads to reorganize and cut frivolous costs. They didn't. So he ordered it again. They still didn't. So he ordered it again. Still no action.

What was wrong? They were protecting their turf. They wanted their personal kingdoms to be as large as possible to make them look as important as possible. What did Iacocca do about it? He fired every one of the division heads.

In the winter of 1998, Boris Yeltsin, President of Russia, fired his entire cabinet. Why? He'd given them years and years and years to downsize their personal communistic kingdoms. They refused. He replaced them with younger, more free-enterprise-oriented people.

Expecting an organization to self-destruct from the top down will not happen.

However, over the years, some individual ministers have actually done just that. They have broken away from their denominational affiliations. Here's the story of a few of them as reported in a restoration magazine:

A minister named Mr. Crenshaw broke away from his denomination to become simply a New Testament Christian. These are his words: "October 5, 1984 marked both a beginning and an end. It ended a year of serious soul-searching and many sleepless nights which stemmed from an intense, disturbing study of the Bible.

"It ended a three-year pastorate in the _____ church which was judged by all to be a highly successful one. It began on the other hand, a new life in Christ and a new ministry, this time in the church of our Lord. And it began a set of circumstances which some would label problems, but others opportunities.

"Worth it, it was, and will ever be. But the costs were more dear than I had even anticipated. First, of course, this decision cost me my job, which was my total livelihood, my only visible means of support in a tough financial time. Second, my convictions compelled me to leave a congregation which I dearly loved. Also my union with the church of Christ brought fierce opposition which in turn would cause me to endure much persecution. But was not the only one who had to suffer, as my family and friends were persecuted as well, as a result of my move. It costs to do what is right.

"But it must be noted here that God did not desert me. As stated earlier, I had a peace of mind which I had never had before. But God blessed me in other practical ways. First, he took care of my material needs, and upon doing so, he lifted a great burden from my heart, in that my financial responsibility was great.

"Second, although I left a congregation I dearly loved and still love, I went to a congregation which really took me in and loved me, which meant a great deal.

"Third, in light of the persecution, God gave me great opportunities to return good for evil, thus not only silencing much of the idle conversation, but also opening many doors to study the Bible with people outside of Christ as they viewed my sincerity. God takes care of those who take a stand for the Truth.

"So, what things caused these changes in my life? This has been difficult for some to understand, as I now believe in the same Lord Jesus Christ which I always have. I believe in the same infallible and inerrant Bible that I always have. I have always believed in the virgin birth, the reality of Heaven and Hell, and the preceding judgment. And I have always seen the church as a local, autonomous body. Much of my thinking has not changed.

"The changes did not come about because of incidentals or a matter of expedience. I did not leave my former faith and fellowship because I ceased to love my former brethren - we have the best of relationships, speaking of the people I worked directly with as their pastor. I did not leave it because I became miffed at some sentiment of the _____ convention, though I disagreed with many of the _____ practices.... Instead, my change was due strictly to conviction of what the Word of God teaches....

"I must wear the name of my Lord. And I can't in good conscience give coequal billing to any man-made religious name in relation to the name of Jesus Christ....I hurt inside when I think of all those I have taught wrongly....Tearing down presuppositions in order to see clearly God's Truth is a difficult task at best, but can be done with humble, honest and sincere hearts." [26]

So, encourage your pastor or minister or preacher or whatever title he goes by. Pulling out of denominationalism may mean him losing a well-respected position in the hierarchy of that denomination. The persecution he may face will be much greater than what ordinary members do. Encourage him and let him know he will not lose his job and the members of his congregation will stand by him.

Newness of Life

Discuss withdrawing from denominationalism as a congregation. Then pray, pray, pray. Pray together. Have chain prayers. Have prayer groups. Pray each hour of a 24-hour day. Watch your tolerance for each other grow. Watch your differences melt into insignificance in the shadow of the cross.

If you want a reliable sign on how to change, contact some neighbors to your church building and offer to provide breakfast some Saturday morning in exchange for them candidly telling you what they think of church in general and yours in specific. This is called a focus group. Ask for permission to record their comments for the entire congregation. Then write them up and talk about them as a congregation.

Finally, give it a try. Set aside one Sunday where you will follow only what the New Testament specifically says for the church, not what it infers or you wish it had said. If the Bible is silent about something, omit it.

At this first service, hand out a bulletin to everyone explaining what will happen so no one is caught by surprise. Then read an appropriate scripture before each activity such as before the singing, before the praying, before the Lord's Supper, etc. This way everyone will understand it is specifically represented in the God's Word. And include these scripture in your bulletin where it lists each separate activity so everyone can go home and look it up and study it in private.

Then invite friends to come.

Remember when you first turned your life over to God? Remember your excitement? Maybe it's been hard to get that excited since then. But now, using the exciting first-century pattern, the New Testament pattern, you will have a new excitement. For now, your Sunday morning services will reflect God's love for everyone through you.

This is the time to invite friends. While you're still excited. "We tried something new in church last Sunday. It was unbelievable! I felt so warm and so wanted. I know it's going to change my life for the better. Go with me next Sunday!"

Many people will say no at first. That is just because they need time to think. The first no never really means no. Give them time to think, then ask them again. Tell, tell, tell. Ask, ask, ask. Your heart will overflow so much when you enter into worship the way Jesus intended it.

Worship that is simple, but dynamic in its simplicity.

Help us, God. We want to worship you. We want to be pleasing to you. Help us do this!

Oh Jesus. We get set in our ways. We think we're already in heaven, and forget to constantly re-examine ourselves. Forgive us for setting ourselves before others. Forgive us for holding back from being the example you want us be.

Forgive our selfishness in the way we worship you, regardless of the lost outsiders and even the lost among us who want to know you too.

Forgive our fears. Help us understand that we cannot be "more than conquerors through you" unless we have something to conquer. Take us in our weakness, and be our strength.

You are our help and strength. You are our rock of salvation. You are the path we tread, the light that shines it, and our ultimate destination. We fall at your feet unworthy. We fall at your feet whispering "Thank you."

ENDNOTES

[1]. *The Holy Bible*: New International Version, International Bible Society, 1988. [All Bible references from NIV unless otherwise noted.]

[2]. Wells, H. G., *The Outline of History: The Whole Story of Man*, Vol. I, Book VI, Ch. 28, Garden City Books, Garden City, NY, Pg. 438-439.

[3]. Reasoner, *Be One*, pg. 264-265.

[4]. Luther, Martin, *"Admonition Against Insurrection,"* 1522.

[5]. Wesley, John, *Notes on the New Testament*

[6]. Wells, H. G. *The Outline of History* Vol I, Book VI, Part XXXI, Pg. 544-545.

[7]. Goldin, Hyman E., translator, *Code of Jewish Law*, Hebrew Publishing Co., N.Y., Vol. I, pg. 125-129.

[8]. Reasoner, N. J., *Be One*, N. D. Elliott, Printer, Salem, OR, 1928, (Restoration Reprint Library, College Press, Joplin, MO. December 1926,) pg. 252-253.

[9]. Wells, H. G., *The Outline of History* Book VI, Ch. 28, pg.438-439.

[10]. Reasoner, *Be One*, pg. 233.

[11]. Reasoner, *Be One*, pg. 233 and 236.

[12]. George, David L., *The Family Book of Best Loved Poems*, Hanover House, Garden City, NY, 1952, pg. 400-401

[13]. Reasoner, *Be One*, pg. 280.

[14]. Wells, H. G., *The Outline of History*, Book VI, Ch. 28, pg. 432.

[15]. Allen, Roland, *The Spontaneous Expansion of the church*, Wm. B. Eerdmans Publishing co., Grand Rapids, MI, 1962, pg. 43-48.

[16]. Allen, *The Spontaneous Expansion of the church*, pg. 98 and 106.

[17]. Allen, *The Spontaneous Expansion of the church*, pg. 124.

[18]. Allen, *The Spontaneous Expansion of the church*, pg. 7-8.

[19]. Allen, *The Spontaneous Expansion of the church*, pg. 12-13.

[20]. Allen, *The Spontaneous Expansion of the church*, pg. 15-16.

[21]. Allen, *The Spontaneous Expansion of the church*, pg. 156-157.

[22]. Reasoner, *Be One*, pg 269.

[23]. Reasoner, *Be One*, pg. 248.

[25]. Reasoner, *Be One*, pg. 257.

[26]. *Restoration Leadership Quarterly*, "The Spotlight," Winter 1985, pg. 3.

7. *FORWARD! BACK TO THE FIRST CENTURY*

United We Stand!

Another chapter for our denominational friends

Thank you, Jesus, for your example. You gave up everything and you gave everything. You brought nothing with you, but you opened the door to all things. You fought in the flesh so we could see your Spirit at work. You stayed loyal to truth and your Father and even demanded it of others. Then you died for us so we could live. How can we thank you enough?

When today's seniors were children, there were all kinds of "sins" that we do not consider sins today. For example, it was a sin to eat at a restaurant that served liquor or go to pool halls because they always served liquor. After all, drunkenness is a sin. It was a sin to play with dice and spot cards because they were used to gamble away men's paychecks and their families would go without. It was a sin for women not to wear hats in church because they weren't being humble enough.

What changed? It got so all the restaurants served liquor, so we'd never go out to eat if we stayed away from them. Pool tables started to be set up in homes and even in church halls for the young people. Monopoly and other innocent board games were invented where dice and playing cards were used. And women started getting fancy hairdos they didn't want mashed down with hats.

Did sin change? No. God never changes and he is the one who decides what a sin is. Of course, sin is anything that ultimately hurts us. Our Creator was not picking on us when he created his lists of things for us to do and not do. Our Creator always wanted the best for us.

But our perception of what would lead us into sin changed. We decided we could eat among people who drank without being tempted to get drunk ourselves. We decided we could play with dice and playing cards without being tempted to gamble. We decided women could go hatless to church without being tempted to usurp authority.

But people who went to church did not change easily or quickly. They changed only when they began to be ready in their private lives for change.

People from every type religious background are reading this book. In fact, you are probably attending church where the members come from many religious backgrounds. Some of you have even given up attending church anywhere.

One ever-lingering problem is how to determine what is a sin and what isn't, so that our worship services are approved by both the congregation and God.

Oh, Jesus. Our sins caused your death. We are so sorry. And every time we sin, we crucify you anew. I study the Bible a lot so I can identify sin and so there aren't so many for you to forgive. We love you.

But I Thought the Bible Said That

Remember the apple in the Garden of Eden? At least, that's what we were all told when we were young. Probably most people reading this book have since come to realize the Bible never mentions an apple. Genesis 3:6 merely says, "fruit of the tree was good for food....she took some and ate it." Were we mistaken? Yes. Honestly mistaken. But mistaken.

How about angels marrying people? Weren't some of us told that the sons of God mentioned in Genesis 6:1 were angels, even though sons of God never means that anywhere else in the Bible, and even though Jesus himself said in Mark 12:25 "neither marry nor be given in marriage...like the angels in heaven." Were we mistaken? Yes. Honestly mistaken. But mistaken.

Can forty days rain flood the world? Ask anyone who lives in the northwest U.S. or southwest Canada. It rains months at a time there. Genesis 7:11 says, "[a] all the springs of the great deep [ocean] burst forth, [b] and the floodgates of the heavens were opened." Genesis 7:24 says, "the waters prevailed upon the earth 150 days." Some Christian scientists believe there was a tidal wave created by the springs in the ocean that lasted 150 days. Now that would flood the world! Were we mistaken? Yes. Honestly mistaken. But mistaken.

Then there's the burning of Sodom and Gomorrah. We were always told God destroyed these two cities, and this is true. But there were two other cities destroyed with them. Deuteronomy 29:23 says Admah and Zeboiim were also destroyed with them. Did people purposely deceive us? No. These other cities certainly aren't listed in the Genesis account. It's an easy mistake to make. Were we mistaken? Yes. Honestly mistaken. But mistaken.

How about Moses' Ten Commandments. There were indeed ten commandments written on two stone tablets. But all anyone has to do is try to plod through Leviticus to see that there were over 600 commandments, not just ten. Leviticus starts out, "The Lord called to Moses.... 'Speak to the Israelites.' " And yet, even though we know about them, we don't usually make the connection. They were all part of the Law of Moses. Were we mistaken? Yes. Honestly mistaken. But mistaken.

Many have trouble understanding how a good God could randomly select territory belonging to another nation and have them killed just so the new Jewish nation could move into their "Promised Land." However, it was not random and wasn't just a killing spree. Four hundred years earlier, God told Abraham in Genesis 15:16 that his descendants were to punish the Amorites for their sins which will have reached their "full measure" by then. Were we mistaken? Yes. Honestly mistaken. But mistaken.

We refer to the psalms that David wrote, regardless of which psalm it was. Even though he wrote most of them, he did not write near all of them. Asaph wrote many, Solomon wrote some, Ethan, Moses, Babylonian exiles. Just look at the subtitles in that book. We've just always assumed David wrote them all. Were we mistaken? Yes. Honestly mistaken. But mistaken.

What about the star in the east? How many of us have referred to that in regards to Jesus' birth? However, the star was not in the east. The wise men were in the east seeing the star where

Jesus was in the west (Matthew 2:1). Also, we assume the star lasted until the wise men showed up. But Matthew 2:9-10 tells us that after they left Jerusalem upon being told the king was to be born in Bethlehem, "the star they had seen in the east went ahead of them....When they saw the star, they were overjoyed." Were we mistaken? Yes. Honestly mistaken. But mistaken.

How about Jesus' bar mitzvah, calling a boy to the Torah, at age twelve? There was never any such ceremony in Bible times. It is nowhere in the Bible. This ceremony is to celebrate a boy's thirteenth birthday, not twelfth, and is not found in any Jewish writings until the Middle Ages, centuries after Bible times. Check your encyclopedia. It's all there. Were we mistaken? Yes. Honestly mistaken. But mistaken.

Consider all the times we have turned to Psalm 23 for comfort. Yet, all that changed for Christians. Luke 1:78-79 says that the coming of Jesus is to bring the sun to those in the shadow of death. To the Christian, there is no darkness in that valley. Wow! How could we have missed it? Were we mistaken? Yes. Honestly mistaken. But mistaken.

Then there's the so-called "fact" that Joseph died during Jesus' boyhood. It's easy to come to that conclusion because of mentioning some of Mary's activities during Jesus' adulthood, and Jesus' having the Apostle John take care of her after his death. However, John 6:42 says " 'IS this not Jesus, the son of JOSEPH, WHOSE FATHER and mother WE KNOW?' " That is present tense. This was said the spring before Jesus was crucified. It could be that Joseph was sick during Jesus' ministry and did not get out. If he did die during Jesus' last year, can you imagine his turmoil in deciding whether or not to return Joseph to health? What a whole new train of thoughts arise from this. Were we mistaken? Yes. Honestly mistaken. But mistaken.

So now that we've admitted we can be mistaken sometimes after all, is it possible we've been mistaken about some very critical things in the Bible?

There are people today who say we should keep the Laws of Moses where they concern worship. But Colossians 2:14 says God "canceled the written code with its regulations...nailing it to the cross." Hebrews 8:13 says, "By calling this covenant 'new,' he has made the first one obsolete; and what is obsolete and aging will soon disappear." Hebrews 9:1 goes on to say, "Now the first covenant had regulations for worship." So, if we take part of the Old Testament worship, we have to accept burning incense, having a high priest, offering animal sacrifices, and all the other regulations too.

Oh God, I thought I knew the Bible better than that. I thought I was a good student. What else have I gotten mixed up on?

Re-educating our Consciences

Have we been doing things in our worship services that we were told not to do in the Word of God? That's a sin of commission. For instance, adding lemon pie to the Lord's Supper would be a sin of commission. Have we been omitting things in our worship services we are told to do in the Word of God? That's a sin of omission. For instance, eliminating prayer would be a sin of omission.

But this is not always a simple thing to come to terms with.

It is a sin to go against our consciences (Romans 14:22-23). Our consciences have been trained. They may have been trained rightly or wrongly.

For example, Christians in the city of Corinth had previously worshipped idols. Before their conversion, they had offered meat sacrifices to their god and then had eaten them as part of their religious rite. (The Jews did the same thing in their worship of God under the Law of Moses; for instance, eating the Passover Lamb in their homes that they had previously sacrificed at the temple.)

In Corinth, apparently there were more sacrifices than the people could eat, so the rest was sold in the meat market. We know that idols are nothing but wood or stone carved by man and have no life or power in them. But for the person who used to worship that lifeless statue, it was a sin to eat the meat because, to them, they were worshipping that idol. They had not completely retrained their consciences.

Paul warned, "Some people are still so accustomed to idols that when they eat such food they think of it as having been sacrificed to an idol, and since their conscience is weak, it is defiled....Be careful, however, that the exercise of your freedom does not become a stumbling block to the weak.

"For if anyone with a weak conscience sees you who have this knowledge eating in an idol's temple, won't he be emboldened to eat what has been sacrificed to idols? So this weak brother, for whom Christ died, is destroyed by your knowledge. When you sin against your brothers in this way and wound their weak conscience, you sin against Christ" (1st Corinthians 8:7-12).

A modern example of this might be people who are used to bowing down before a cross. But later they realize this is a form of idolatry. If a congregation has a cross in its building and there are a lot of people who used to bow down to it and would be offended by it, perhaps the cross should be taken down.

In medieval times, people died at the stake rather than bow to or kiss a cross, or even make the sign of a cross.

Fox's Book of Martyrs tells of Francis Gamba in Italy who, in 1553, was sentenced to execution for his beliefs. Just before lighting the fire, a monk held a cross up to him, and he said, "My mind is so full of the real merits and goodness of Christ that I want not a piece of senseless stick to put me in mind of Him." For that, a hole was carved through his tongue and then he was burned alive. [1]

John Willes in Ireland in the 16th century was flogged because he refused to kneel to the cross or to make the sign of the cross on his forehead. [2]

Near that same time in the Netherlands, a widow named Wendelinuta, was sentenced to be burned at a stake for her beliefs. At the place of execution, a monk held a cross to her and said that if she would kiss it, she would be saved. She answered, "I worship no wooden god, but the eternal God who is in heaven." Thereupon, she was strangled and burned to ashes. [3]

In 1560 in Rome, Italy, an old man was condemned to execution for refusing to be part of the Roman Catholic church.

When they fastened him to the stake, a priest held a crucifix out to him, and he replied, "If you do not take that idol from my sight, you will constrain me to spit upon it." Then he reminded the monk of the first and second commandments to refrain from idolatry. Thereupon he was burned to death. [4]

So, while it is possible to look at a cross without worshipping it, some religions have done just that. People coming out of those religions are offended by an image of the cross for that reason. They should not be forced to look at the cross on display because of our lack of sensitivity to their conscience.

What is the best way to re-educate a conscience? Paul, in Romans 9:1, said, "I speak the truth in Christ - I am not lying, my conscience confirms it in the Holy Spirit."

Jesus was the Word that lived a perfect life (John 1:1, 14; 2nd Corinthians 5:21). Jesus said, "I am the way, the truth, the life." Therefore, the "truth in Christ" would be the Word. Furthermore, Jesus called the Holy Spirit the Spirit of Truth, and said that God's Word was the Truth (John 14:6, 16f; 17:17).

Therefore, having one's conscience confirmed in the Holy Spirit is not the result of following an emotion but rather the result of following the Bible, the Word of Truth. This, of course, will lead to emotion; but the emotion does not do the leading.

God, I'm trying. But my conscience was formed so long ago. It's so hard to change. Help me.

To Compromise....

But it takes time to study and learn everything God has to say on a topic. If we plunge into things too fast that are offensive to people, or if we suddenly keep people from doing things they always thought were holy, we could play a part in searing the conscience of someone.

Do we refuse to meet with people because they have not had time and/or opportunity to search the Scriptures about their beliefs?

North America is the last stronghold of Christianity in the entire world. Islam is the fastest-growing religion, and it is everywhere, including North America. We are also being bombarded by the New Age movement, a movement that says the god of the Buddhists, the god of the Hindus, the god of the pantheists, the god of the witches, the God of the Christians, the god of Islam is all the same God because they are all man-made religions anyway. We need to strengthen each other as much as possible.

Fighting from within will destroy us the rest of the way. The first-century church thrived when people fought them from without, even to the death. But fighting within will destroy us. In fact, fighting from within is one of the causes people completely leave Christianity.

When there are bills before the legislature challenging our faith, do we check on each other's beliefs on how they interpret grace or the thousand-year reign before banding together to oppose legislation that will hurt our nation?

When there is a National Day of Prayer, do we refuse to participate because we might not believe everything the same way someone else who is praying does? God knows all. He will sort it all out.

When there is a March for Jesus, do we refuse to march because we might not believe everything the same way the person next to us believes? How could the people on the sidewalk possibly know this? All they know is that Jesus is being magnified—no more, no less.

If we were threatened with imprisonment or even death for believing Jesus is the Son of God, would we refuse because someone else was going to be imprisoned or executed with us who didn't believe all the details that we do?

Should we try compromise? Just what can we compromise on and not compromise on? Compromise is hard. It's frightening. We're talking about eternity here. How many chances do we dare take in displeasing God? In the next section we will discuss how far we can go with compromise before it becomes heresy. But for now, we will look at ways compromise was practiced in Bible times.

The Jews certainly had some major problems to face when they were converted to Christianity.

1. To Jews, Saturdays were considered holy (Exodus 20:8-11; 31:13-16). Now, as Christians, Sundays were considered holy (Acts 20:7; Matthew 28:1).

How did they handle it? Since their 24-hour days ran from sundown to sundown, as soon as the Sabbath was over, for instance 6:00 PM, they began keeping Sunday holy, for instance 7:00 PM.

2. Jews had to offer innumerable types of sacrifices for many different types of sins (Leviticus ch. 1 - 7). Now, as Christians, they had to refrain from that because Jesus had been sacrificed for their sins once for all (Hebrews 9:23-28).

How did they handle it? Every Sunday they gathered together to have the Lord's Supper which they did in remembrance of his sacrifice, and to contemplate their sins (Acts 20:7, 1st Corinthians 11:23-32).

3. Jews had to go to the temple three times a year for special religious feasts, Passover (Feast of Unleavened Bread), and so on. Now, as Christians, the feasts were unnecessary because Jesus brought us out of slavery to sin, Jesus gave a new law, and Jesus was the final sacrifice to atone for our sins.

How did they handle it? They took advantage of those old feast times and went to the temple to explain how Jesus had become their Passover Lamb (1st Corinthians 5:7) and other such Christian beliefs. And Christians living in Jerusalem went to the temple every day (Acts 2:46-47) to explain their new-found faith in their new-found Savior, Jesus.

4. Jewish male babies had to be circumcised as a testimony to carry on to the next generation the promise of God to be their King of kings (Genesis 17:10-12). One of the derogatory terms the Jews had used for Gentiles was "the uncircumcised." Now, as Christians, circumcision was unnecessary, for the promised King of kings had finally come.

How did they handle it? The apostles and elders in

Jerusalem decided to not place that burden on the Gentile believers (Acts 15:10-11, 19). Was this easy for the Jews? No. Paul told the Jews in several letters to quit pressuring the Gentile Christians to be circumcised (1st Corinthians 7:18-20; Galatians 6: 12-13).

However, in order to not offend the Jews to whom Timothy was preaching the gospel, Paul circumcised Timothy, whose father was a full-blooded Greek and apparently kept his Jewish mother from carrying this out in his infancy (Acts 16:1-3). But Paul refused to circumcise Greek Titus because Jewish Christians were insisting Titus do so in order to be saved (Galatians 2:3).

Although Paul sometimes kept an old Jewish regulation (see below), he told other Christians they did not have to because it meant nothing anymore to God. It is something he occasionally did by himself. It never became something he insisted others do.

5. Whenever Jews asked God for such things as traveling mercies, or whenever they wanted to dedicate themselves to God for a special period of time, they made a vow which they paid for at the temple and let their hair grow (see chapter on "Giving" in the other book of this series, *Worship the First-Century Way*). At the end of the vow, they shaved their heads. Now, as Christians, they did not have to pay for their prayers. They went directly to God free of charge, for Jesus had paid the ultimate price.

How did they handle it? On a visit to Jerusalem, the apostles and elders there apparently gave Paul some bad advice, but meant well by it. They encouraged Paul to pay the expenses of some other Jewish Christians to complete their vows and for Paul to do the same himself. So they went to the temple and did so. But a week later, Paul was falsely accused by the very Jews he was trying to appease (Acts 21-26). As a result he was arrested, imprisoned a couple years, and finally sent to Rome for more imprisonment and trial.

6. Jews had to go through priests to take care of all ceremonies (Leviticus). Now, as Christians, they could participate in all ceremonies directly.

How did they handle it? They were continually told that every Christian is a priest (1st Peter 2:5-9; Revelation 1:6 and 5:10 and 20:6) and they must offer their bodies as daily sacrifices

(Romans 12:1).

Paul said in 1st Corinthians 9:20-22, "To the Jews I become like a Jew, to win the Jews. ...To those who not have the law, I become like one not having the law....To the weak I became weak, to win the weak. I have become all things to all men, so that by all possible means I might save some."

Paul spent a lot of time discussing this problem of conscience with the church at Rome.

"Accept him whose faith is weak, without passing judgment on disputable matters. One man's faith allows him to eat everything, but another man, whose faith is weak, eats only vegetables. The man who eats everything must not look down on him who does not, and the man who does not eat everything must not condemn the man who does, for God has accepted him. Who are you to judge someone else's servant? To his own master he stands or falls. And he will stand, for the Lord is able to make him stand" (Romans 14:1-4).

There was a congregation a long time ago in Arkansas that decided to merge with another one because their beliefs were almost identical, but not quite. They disagreed with what to do with the contribution and the church building. The more conservative group did not want their contribution going to help works of other congregations because they felt this was allowing elders of one congregation to be over elders of another congregation. They also did not believe dinners and parties should be held in the church building.

Neither concern was a matter of salvation. The two congregations decided they should honor the more conservative ones. Therefore, none of the regular Sunday contributions went outside of their merged congregation. Whenever a dinner or party was held in the building, it was mentioned but not emphasized; those who went home due to their conscience were never taunted for not staying.

Thank you for your Word, God. These examples really help me. The Jewish Christians had to make a lot of changes in the way they worship. If all I had to change was two or three things, it would be nothing compared with what they went through.

The Secret: Conservative

There is a wonderful secret to getting along. Go along with the more conservative group and the rest work around them. Who are the conservatives?

Primarily, conservatives are the ones who (1) take practices in the Bible literally, and (2) don't practice anything not commanded or modeled by the apostles. Those who want to add to the practices of the conservatives can do so before or after a regular service, or in private.

Making concessions is very difficult, especially the first time. After all, we're talking about our salvation. For people who even subconsciously believe other Christians have to answer to them instead of to God it is extremely difficult. One must pray about it. After all, Jesus told a man to carry his bed on the Sabbath.

Perhaps we should make this our motto:

In matters of salvation and worship—unity.
In matters of opinion—liberty.
In all things—love.

For example, if some believe in both foot washing and instrumental music and others believe in neither, could not a concession be made? Singing without an instrument is not considered a sin by anyone, so that concession is easy. On the other hand, foot washing never hurt anyone, so perhaps those who do believe it could do so in their homes, thus making that concession easy too.

Paul continues in Romans 14:5-8: "One man considers one day more sacred than another; another man considers every day alike. Each one should be fully convinced in his own mind. He who regards one day as special, does so to the Lord. He who eats meat, eats to the Lord, for he gives thanks to God; and he who abstains, does so to the Lord and gives thanks to God. For none of us lives to himself alone and none of us dies to himself alone. If we live, we live to the Lord; and if we die, we die to the Lord. So, whether we live or die, we belong to the Lord...."

As discussed in the other book in this series (Worship the First-Century Way) on the Lord's Supper, Acts 20:7 says the early Christians met on the first day of every week (Sunday) for the specific purpose of breaking bread in the religious sense. But what about people who want to keep Easter as a special time once a year? Continue to keep the Lord's Supper every week. Then once a year, devote your entire service to the Lord's Supper — though not necessarily on the day denominations and Catholics believe Easter must be kept.

Congregations get together every year to thank God for their blessings on Thanksgiving. The Bible does not tell us to keep Thanksgiving. It just is not there. However, as long as we are continuing to thank God every week in some way for his blessings, the congregation could spend extra time one of those weeks thanking God. The one special day is not to take the place of all the other days of thanksgiving.

Paul continues, "....For this very reason, Christ died and returned to life so that he might be the Lord of both the dead and the living. You, then, why do you judge your brother? Or why do you look down on your brother? For we will all stand before God's judgment seat. It is written, 'As surely as I live, says the Lord, every knee will bow before me; every tongue will confess to God.' So then, each of us will give an account of himself to God" (Romans 14:9-12).

There are some things mentioned in the Bible that some Christians think were meant to be kept as a ceremony. Other people think they were meant for practical purposes. For example, Jesus washed the apostles' feet when he instituted the Lord's Supper (John 13:1-14). In 1st Timothy 5:9-10, the church is told to support widows with no family if they are over 60, were faithful to their husband, and were known for her good works such as raising children, showing hospitality, washing saints' feet, helping people in trouble, and devoting themselves to good deeds.

Some Christians believe anointing a sick person's head with oil is ceremonial while most others believe it is practical. James 5:14-15 says, "Is anyone of you sick? He should call the elders of the church to pray over him and anoint him with oil in the name of the Lord. And the prayer offered in faith will make the sick person well; the Lord will raise him up."

Most Christians tend to believe such anointing was for medicinal purposes. When Jesus talked about the good Samaritan who helped the man robbed and beaten along the road, the Samaritan "went to him and bandaged his wounds, pouring on oil and wine" (Luke 10:34). Anointing and pouring are the same thing.

However, if there are people who come into a congregation whose consciences have been trained to believe this is ceremonial, once again the more conservatives should be honored. But if they would like to pour oil on the heads of whichever of the sick desire this for ceremonial purposes in their home, they would not be hurting anyone.

Paul continues, "Therefore let us stop passing judgment on one another. Instead, make up your mind not to put any stumbling block or obstacle in your brother's way. As one who is in the Lord Jesus, I am fully convinced that no food is unclean in itself. But if anyone regards something as unclean, then for him it is unclean. If your brother is distressed because of what you eat, you are no longer acting in love. Do not by your eating destroy your brother for whom Christ died.

"Do not allow what you consider good to be spoken of as evil. For the kingdom of God is not a matter of eating and drinking, but of righteousness, peace and joy in the Holy Spirit, because anyone who serves Christ in this way is pleasing to God and approved by men (Romans 14:13-18).

There are groups who think going to church once each Sunday is enough. However, there are people who sometimes have to work on Sunday morning, or are sick on Sunday morning, or have some other unavoidable hindrance on Sunday morning.

According to 1st Corinthians 11:33, right after Paul spent the previous 32 verses talking about the Lord's Supper, he said, "So then, my brothers, when you come together to eat, wait for each other." Returning to church in the evening so people who missed in the morning can take of the Lord's Supper among other Christians is commendable.

So they need to attend church on Sunday evening to keep the Lord's Supper on the first day of every week. These morning absentees could go to another room in the church building on Sunday evenings to partake of it while the remainder of the congregation sings some songs. Or they could stay with the rest of the congregation and be served while everyone else is respectfully quiet.

There are others who believe only a church officer such as a bishop is allowed to hand them the communion. If someone feels strongly about this, until they are re-educated more fully, it wouldn't hurt for an elder to accommodate this person temporarily. After all, ushers have been putting the communion into the hands and mouths of the sick and palsied for many years and it was not a sin.

Paul cautions, "Let us therefore make every effort to do what leads to peace and to mutual edification. Do not destroy the work of God for the sake of food. All food is clean, but it is wrong for a man to eat anything that causes someone else to stumble. It is better not to eat meat or drink wine or to do anything else that will cause your brother to fall.

"So whatever you believe about these things keep between yourself and God. Blessed is the man who does not condemn himself by what he approves. But the man who has doubts is condemned if he eats, because his eating is not from faith; and everything that does not come from faith is sin" (Romans 14:19-23).

There are some people who love a good choir. But the New Testament says every Christian should sing (see the other book in this series, *Worship the First-Century Way*. Still others believe God called them to sing solos.

With honoring the more conservative ones of the congregation, during the main worship period, everyone would participate in the singing. But the male soloists could lead congregational singing. And rather than singing in the place of the congregation, both male and female soloists could sing for funerals, weddings, in nursing homes, hospitals, for special groups, and to shut-ins.

We must never destroy those for whom Christ died (Romans 14:15). If the more conservative ones in the congregation believe something is wrong, they should not be forced to witness it or participate in it.

Everyone in the congregation with more liberal beliefs must agree to not approach the conservatives to try to talk them into their added belief. We must trust human nature. We must maintain unity. In unity is strength.

Everyone must be honored with the amount of faith they have at the time. After all, if someone is going through a great deal of personal turmoil at home, just attending on Sunday morning and asking for prayers may be all they can handle. Foot washing may be the farthest from their minds. We must not burden them with too much.

God, I never thought of it this way. This really helps. Thank you for your Word. I really do want to honor it. And I want to honor those you love. Help us understand each other better.

How Far is Too Far?

When does a congregation quit being accepted by God? Revelation 2 and 3 point this out with seven congregations, all of which Jesus was about to disown if they didn't change their ways.

The church in Ephesus was full of good works, did not tolerate wicked men, tested and rejected those claiming to be apostles, endured hardships, never grew weary, and hated Nicolaitans (explained below). BUT, they were doing all this either because it was fun or out of legalism, but not out of love. **A congregation with no love** is not accepted by God.

The church in Smyrna endured afflictions, poverty, and slander by Jews. Further, they were about to endure imprisonment and even executions. In such a state, this congregation must have drawn very close. They had nothing to brag about but Jesus. God had nothing against them.

The church in Pergamum remained true to Jesus even where "Satan has his throne," did not renounce faith in Jesus even when one of their members was put to death. BUT, they ate food sacrificed to idols and were sexually immoral. Further, they upheld Nicholaitans. Nicholas means conqueror or controller; laity means the commoner. They'd developed a clergy-laity system and let their leaders get by with it. **A congregation that tolerates idolatry, immorality and a separate clergy** is not accepted by God.

The church in Thyatira performed deeds of love and faith, and did more of it all the time. BUT, they tolerated sexual immorality, eating food sacrificed to idols, and a prophetess who taught "deep secrets" (occult). **A congregation that tolerates immorality, idolatry and New Age views** is not accepted by God.

The church in Sardis did some good deeds. BUT they were dead, asleep because they were not doing enough good deeds. **A congregation that does not center activities around good deeds** is not accepted by God.

The church in Philadelphia had many good deeds, kept their faith even in weakness, remained loyal despite pressure from Jewish unbelievers, and endured all this patiently. God had nothing against them.

The church in Laodicea had no good points. Their deeds were done haphazardly. They were lukewarm. Instead they bragged about their wealth. **A Congregation that is centered around O.T. type materialism instead of good works** is not accepted by God.

To recap, then, what types of congregations are not acceptable to God? Those who....
1. ...have no love.
2. ...tolerate those who do not believe in Jesus.
3. ...tolerate immorality.
4. ...have a clergy-laity system.
5. ...do not emphasize and carry out good works.
6. ...are known primarily for their big building and important members.

God, this is a real eye-opener. I'd heard so many things that I thought God would hate or love. Your Word is so clear. Thank you for caring enough to write it for us.

....Or Not to Compromise

But there is a limit to compromise. If we compromise too far, we can get involved in heresy. Heresy, sectarianism (denominationalism), and choice come from the same word in Greek, *haimorrhoeo, haireomai, hairesis*, depending on how the word is used.

Technically, the word heresy in its simplest form means choice, and therefore is not necessarily good or bad. For instance, Jesus was chosen to be God's servant on earth (Matthew 12:18); Paul had trouble choosing whether to prefer being on earth to preach or going to heaven to see Jesus (Philippians 1:22); God chose Christians to be saved through his divine plan (2nd Thessalonians 2:13); and Moses chose to be mistreated rather than stay royalty (Hebrews 11:25).

All of these examples of choice (*hairesis*) involved life-or-death situations. None of the choices involved anything simplistic. And none of these choices were made on the spur of the moment. They were made after weighing the evidence.

Furthermore, if groups of people make the same choice and it involves religion, the group is called choosers or sectarians.

Acts 5:17; 15:5, and 26:5 all refer to the sects of the Jews, either the Sadducees who did not believe in a literal resurrection of the dead but also believed people should follow just the Law of Moses, or the Pharisees who did believe in the literal resurrection of the dead but also believed people should follow priestly traditions/creeds as just as holy and binding as the Bible.

When Christianity first began, it, too, was considered a sect of the Jews. In Acts 24:5, the Jews in Jerusalem referred to Paul's teaching on behalf of "the Nazarene sect," of course referring to Jesus being from Nazareth. In verse 14, Paul referred to it as the sect called "the Way." Even the Jews in Rome referred to "this sect"

(Acts 28:22).

Thus far, heresy has been identified with private decisions and group decisions. What about decisions an individual tries to FORCE ON groups of people? These are what are normally translated "heresy" in the Bible. These are the kinds of choices that are sinful.

In instances below where the entire passage is quoted, the word translated from this Greek word for heresy is italicized. (In the KJV, these italicized words are translated "heresy".)

Misapplication of a ritual is heresy. In 1st Corinthians 11:17-19 Paul says there were divisions regarding how to keep the Lord's Supper because they had turned them into large feasts, kind of like potluck dinners where the poorer members couldn't come because they couldn't bring their share of the food. Paul concluded that these *differences* [heresies] "show which of you have God's approval."

Hateful attitudes rubbing off on others is heresy. Galatians 5:19-21 lists works of the flesh. Most involving "heresy" are in verse 20—hatred, discord, jealousy, fits of rage, selfish ambition, dissensions, *factions* [heresies].

Just before he died, Peter described and warned about heresy in his second letter 1:15 - 3:2. It is interesting that it has been in Peter's name that many heresies have come about, yet he is the one who warned about it so vehemently.

"I think it is right to refresh your memory as long as I live....And I will make every effort to see that after my departure you will always be able to remember these things...." (1:15)

Denying Jesus is Lord is heresy. "....But there were also false prophets among the people [of Old Testament times], just as there will be false teachers among you. They will secretly introduce destructive heresies, even denying the sovereign Lord who bought them - bringing swift destruction on themselves..." (2:1)

Making up stories of visions or twisting the truth is heresy. "....Many will follow their shameful ways and will bring the way of truth into disrepute. In their greed these teachers will exploit you with stories they have made up. Their condemnation has long been hanging over them, and their destruction has not been sleeping...." (2:2-3)

God will punish such people severely. "....For if God did not spare angels when they sinned, but sent them to hell, putting them into gloomy dungeons to be held for judgment; if he did not spare...the flood...if he condemned the cities of Sodom and Gomorrah by burning..." (2:4-6a)

Despising the authority of the Bible is heresy. "...if this is so, then the Lord knows how to rescue godly men from trials, and to hold the unrighteous for the day of judgment, while continuing their punishment. This is especially true of those who follow the corrupt desire of the sinful nature and despise authority...." (2:9-10a)

Involvement in things the Bible is silent about is heresy. "....Bold and arrogant, these men are not afraid to slander celestial beings; yet even angels, although they are stronger and more powerful, do not bring slanderous accusations against such things in the presence of the Lord. But these men blaspheme in matters they do not understand...." (2:10b-12a)

God will do unto heretics as they have done unto him. "....They are like brute beasts, creatures of instinct, born only to be caught and destroyed, and like beasts they too will perish. They will be paid back with harm for the harm they have done...." (2:12b-13a)

Boastful words to fill personal egos is heresy. "....These men are springs without water and mists driven by a storm. Blackest darkness is reserved for them. For they mouth empty, boastful words and, by appealing to the lustful desires of sinful human nature, they entice people who are just escaping from those who live in error...." (2:17-18)

Taking people back into worldliness or the O.T. Law is heresy. "....They promise them freedom, while they themselves are slaves of depravity—for a man is slave to whatever has mastered him. If they have escaped the corruption of the world by knowing our Lord and Savior Jesus Christ and are again entangled in it and overcome, they are worse off at the end than they were at the beginning. It would have been better for them not to have known the way of righteousness, than to have known it and then to turn their backs on the sacred command that was passed on to them. Of them the proverbs are true: 'A dog returns to its vomit,' and, 'A sow that is washed goes back to her wallowing in the mud.' " (2:19-22)

To recap, then, heresy is...
1. ...misapplication of a ritual.
2. ...hateful attitudes rubbing off on the others.
3. ...denying Jesus is Lord.
4. ...making up stories of visions or twisting the truth.
5. ...involvement in things the Bible is silent about.
6. ...boastful words to fill personal egos.
7. ...taking people back into worldliness.

God, this really helps. Now I understand heresy. Now it is clear. Now I know that sometimes I have been guilty of heresy myself. I'm so sorry, God. I didn't mean to.

Back to the Bible

The only way to avoid heresy is to compare everything with the Bible. "I want you to recall the words spoken in the past by the holy prophets and the command given by our Lord and Savior through your apostles" (2nd Peter 3:2).

How do we do that? In our rushed world today, we are blessed to have a complete index to the Bible the size of an unabridged dictionary called a concordance. By using it, we can look up everything God has to say about any topic. Then we will have the whole story, God's point of view, all we need. There are also searchable concordances on the internet.

Then it is up to us to accept it—no more and no less. Is this easy? Is it easy to give up previous ideas and notions and beliefs? Absolutely not.

Each congregation might list all its beliefs and practices, then go through the New Testament by subject to examine God's opinion of those beliefs and practices. If they are in the Bible, they should be continued. If they are not in the Bible, they should be discontinued. And if, in the process, we find beliefs and practices that are in the Bible but never adhered to by the congregation, these can be adopted.

Is that possible? With an open mind it is. If egos enter in and people become afraid their pet projects or their pet practices or their pet offices are being threatened, it doesn't matter what is in the Bible. People will justify; that is, create a justification of their own rather than of God.

On the other hand, it would be much easier for a congregation to start with a blank sheet of paper and decide that whatever type of worship is found in the New Testament, that will be practiced. If it is not found there, that will not be practiced.

Be careful that only the New Testament is referred to. The Old Testament tells of worship under the Law of Moses. If we copy one way in which they worshipped, we must copy it all — including animal sacrifices (James 2:10). Jesus nailed the old law to the cross (Galatians 3:10; Colossians 2:14).

Therefore, before such a search is made, it must be decided that the congregation will follow the Bible and be willing to give up whatever is necessary with the understanding that their proper beliefs and activities will be elevated in the process.

The apostle Paul warned Timothy shortly before his death, "fight the good fight, holding on to faith and a good conscience. Some have rejected these and so have shipwrecked their faith" (1st Timothy 1:18-19). How does this happen? How do people shipwreck their faith?

"The Spirit clearly says that in later times some will abandon the faith....Such teachings come through hypocritical liars, whose consciences have been seared as with a hot iron. They forbid people to marry and order them to abstain from certain foods" (1st Timothy 4:2-3).

Oh Father, from now on I want to worship you only the way you want to be worshiped. Help me as I search. I want to draw closer to you, not in the ways I want, but in the ways you want. I no longer want to worship my desires, but yours. I love you, God.

A Personal Restoration Movement

There is a difference in a reformation movement and a restoration movement. Reformation is reactionism. In a reformation movement, if the Catholics do something one way, reformers will do it the opposite way.

For example, Catholics use unleavened bread for the Lord's Supper; therefore, reactionaries will use leavened bread for the Lord's Supper. Catholic priests wear ornate vestments; therefore, reactionary leaders will wear plain vestments. Catholics practice baptism for salvation; therefore, reactionaries will eliminate baptism. No one checks to see what God has to say about it in the Bible. They just react to what has been done in the past by others.

Many people and congregations have been involved in a restoration movement without identifying themselves as restorers. Any individual or congregation who insists on only the Bible with no creeds or requirements set forth in its world headquarters is involved in a restoration movement. But a restoration movement can only be carried out with access to the Bible.

Restoration movements have popped up through the centuries. The New Testament church has never really died. (See the chapters on the church through the centuries just in Europe.)

Its history is fascinating. Each movement was its own restoration movement. Restoration movements are spontaneous and local. It is often difficult to find these movements, because they normally did not meddle with what other congregations were doing. They just refused to become the official national religion declared by their parliaments or kings. All they wanted to do was please God and not man.

There are many lonely people out there who think they are the only ones who read the Bible for themselves and the only ones who want to follow it. When I first met a certain man named John, he was one of those people. He had drifted from one church to another, trying to find the church of the first century, the church of the New Testament.

"I finally decided there was no such thing," he said. So he quit going to church anywhere. His frustration was unbelievable.

Then, when we met, he said one day, "What do you think about...?" I gave him my reply, and he suspiciously said, "How did you know that?" I said, "Because the Bible says so right in such-and-such passage."

So he said, "Well, what do you think about...?" I replied to that, his eyes got wide, and he said once again, "How did you know that?" Once again I said, "Because the Bible says so right in such-and-such passage."

He sat down. This was not happening. Not after all those years of searching. He said, "Well, try this one. What do you think about....?" Once more I gave him a reply out of the Bible. He just sat there staring.

Finally he said, "And I thought I was the only one." So I said, "There's a whole congregation I attend that puts the Bible above everything and everyone else." He could hardly believe his ears and immediately began attending.

What was most sad about it is that he had attended a congregation like that which I normally attend and he was put off by it because of the reputation of the minister and some of the members in town. He also said, "All they ever wanted to do was debate." How sad. All those empty years he wasted searching.

Every time we find a restoration movement, we find individuals and congregations who answer only to themselves and to God. Do we need to have a world headquarters to decide what to believe? Do we have to consult with representatives of other congregations to decide what to believe?

Do we have to even check up on other congregations to be sure they conform? Although it is encouraging to know which other congregations there are who are like-minded with us, we do not need to get with them to decide what to believe, nor do we need to get with them to check them out. That is when we get into trouble. That is when we take the place of God.

For an effective restoration movement, we must let loose of control. We must quit trying to control other congregations by attending synods to vote for what we should believe in or pressuring them through church papers or websites. The Bible allows only for such decisions to be made on the congregational level. To be the true church of Christ, the body of people Jesus named after himself, we must follow his instructions through his apostles found in the New Testament. Do we have the courage?

Dear Father in heaven. Sometimes I forget you are the Father and I am the child. Sometimes I want to take your role. Forgive me. Help me let go. Help me concentrate on my own worship, and the worship only of my own congregation. And help us understand as you do.

Holy Wars

"Holy wars" have been fought trying to win over people who did not see a need to change because they did not understand the potential for a greater good by changing.

"Holy wars" were fought to try to win converts. The crusaders went out and murdered Muslims who refused to become Christians. "Holy wars" have also been fought in a sort of civil war, Christians arguing with fellow Christians over often vague points of doctrine.

One way to contain our "holy wars" is to eliminate discussions of opinion.

We get sidetracked from our main purpose of the church's existence — to save souls — in order to argue with each other within our congregation or with people of other denominations. Is winning that important to us? What about cooperation?

It's our arguing that creates our divisiveness. And usually our arguing is a matter of semantics.

1st Timothy 1:3-7; 6:4-5 says false doctrines "promote controversies rather than God's work — which is by faith. The goal of this command is love, which comes from a pure heart and a good conscience and a sincere faith. Some have wandered away from these and turned to meaningless talk. They want to be teachers of the law, but they do not know what they are talking about or what they so confidently affirm."

"....he is conceited and understands nothing. He has an

unhealthy interest in controversies and quarrels about words that result in envy, strife, malicious talk, evil suspicions and constant friction between men of corrupt mind, who have been robbed of the truth and who think that godliness is a means to financial gain."

H. G. Wells, the famous historian, said, "Jesus had called men and women to a giant undertaking, to the renunciation of self, to the new birth into the kingdom of love. The line of least resistance for the flagging convert was to intellectualize himself away from this plain doctrine, this stark proposition, into complicated theories and ceremonies, that would leave his essential self alone....

"Jesus called himself the Son of God and also the Son of man; but he laid little stress on who he was or what he was, and much upon the teachings of the Kingdom....By the fourth century of the Christian Era we find all the Christian communities so agitated and exasperated by torturous and elusive arguments about the nature of God as to be largely negligent of the simpler teachings of charity, service, and brotherhood that Jesus had inculcated." [5]

2nd Timothy 2:23-26 warns, "Don't have anything to do with foolish and stupid arguments, because you know they produce quarrels. And the Lord's servant must not quarrel; instead, he must be kind to everyone, able to teach, not resentful. Those who oppose him he must gently instruct, in the hope that God will grant them repentance leading them to a knowledge of the truth, and that they will come to their senses and escape from the trap of the devil, who has taken them captive to do his will."

Finally, after reminding Christians we were all saved from sin by Jesus Christ, he goes on to say, "But avoid foolish controversies and genealogies and arguments and quarrels about the law, because these are unprofitable and useless. Warn a divisive person once, and then warn him a second time. After that, have nothing to do with him. You may be sure that such a man is warped and sinful; he is self-condemned" (Titus 3:9).

Jehovah God. I fall at your feet, a sinner. I have argued with people in the church about things we both should have remained silent. I've caused you grief and pain. There are so many important things to talk about - like lost souls.

I got sidetracked. I promise to do better.

Matters of Opinion

What makes something a matter of opinion? It is something that cannot be proven, or something that the Bible seems to provide two points of view on which we humans still have not figured out how to reconcile and balance.

The Apostle Paul explained this in his encouraging letter to the church in Rome which consisted of people of all nationalities and religious backgrounds:

"So whatever you believe about these things KEEP BETWEEN YOURSELF AND GOD" (Romans 14:22).

Some hot controversies include once saved, always saved; predestination; premillennialism; end of the world; ordination; closed communion; trinity. We must learn to keep these things to ourselves, regardless of which "side" we are on.

In the 21st century, the church is in jeopardy. Can we stop talking about matters that don't interfere with salvation or worship long enough to unite somehow and return the church to its former strength, or even stronger? All we need to agree on is....

(1) how to be saved/become Christians (so we know who to recognize)

(2) how to worship (because we do that together).

H. G. Wells concluded, "We are bound to recognize that beneath these preposterous refinements of impossible dogmas there lay often a real passion for truth—even if it was truth ill-conceived. Both sides produced genuine martyrs. And the zeal of these controversies...a base and often malicious zeal."[6]

What God through the Apostle Paul said in Philippians 1:15-18 should frame our attitudes toward others claiming Christ:

"It is true that some preach Christ out of envy and rivalry, but others out of goodwill. The latter do so in love, knowing that I am put here [in jail] for the defence of the gospel. The former preach Christ out of selfish ambition, not sincerely, supposing that they can stir up trouble for me while I am in chains. BUT WHAT DOES IT MATTER? The important thing is that in every way, whether from false motives or true, CHRIST IS PREACHED. And because of this I REJOICE!"

Must we be enemies over our opinions? Can we not keep them to ourselves?

I may think that I am strong and you are weak, while you may think you are strong and I am weak. Who is to say who is right? If it has nothing to do with salvation, it could be opinion. God told us, "Accept him whose faith is weak, without passing judgment on disputable matters" (Romans 14:1).

Everyone is at a different place in their Christian maturing process, sometimes because of previous training, sometimes because of age, sometimes because of different backgrounds, sometimes simply because of personality.

Because I make myself go to church four times a week, does that make me spiritually superior to the one who only attends once, but who has converted two people to Christ in the last year compared with my none? Because I read the Bible through every year, does that make me spiritually superior to the one who does not, but who reads selected Scriptures to people in nursing homes? "Who are you [we] to judge someone else's servant. To his own master he stands or falls....So then, each of us will give an account of himself to God" (Romans 14:4, 12).

Father, I'm a sinner just like everyone else. Forgive my arrogance over things that are just a matter of opinion. Help me return to matters that really are important. Help me spend my time, not in arguing with my brothers and sisters, but in snatching people out of the jaws of Satan. I have let you down. I have let the church down. Forgive me, a sinner. I have let the lost down. I promise from now on I will do better.

===

Second-Generation Church Accounts

**About AD 96, Clement wrote in his Epistle to the Corinthians, verse 21, "It is right therefore that we should not be deserters from His will. Let us rather give offence to foolish and senseless men who exalt themselves and boast in the arrogance of their words, than to God. Let us fear the Lord Jesus, whose blood was given for us." [7]

About AD 100, Ignatius wrote in his Epistle to the Ephesians, verse 3, "Even though I am in bonds for the Name's sake, I am not yet perfected in Jesus Christ. Now am I beginning to be a disciple....For I ought to be trained by you for the contest in faith, in abomination, in endurance, in long-suffering." [8]

Soon after, Ignatius wrote in his Epistle to Polycarp, verse 1, "...exhort all men that they may be saved....Suffer all men in love, as also you do. Give yourself to unceasing prayers. Ask for larger wisdom than you have. Be watchful, and keep your spirit from slumbering. Speak to each man severally after the manner of God. Bear the maladies of all." [9]

ENDNOTES

[1]. Forbush, William F, Edit, *Fox's Book of Martyrs*, Zondervan, Grand Rapids, 1968, pg. 103

[2]. *Ibid., pg. 271*

[3] *Ibid.*, pg. 173

[4]. *Ibid., pg. 105*

[5]. Wells, H. G., *The Outline of History*, Garden City Books, Garden City, NY, Doubleday, 1961, Bk 6, Ch. 28, pg. 432

[6]. Wells, Book 6, Pt. 28, pg. 434

[7]. Lightfoot, J. B., *The Apostolic Fathers*, Baker Book House, Grand Rapids, 1965, pg. 22f

[8]. *Ibid.*, pg. 64

[9]. *Ibid.*, pg. 86

About Book II
WORSHIP THE FIRST-CENTURY WAY

Would you like to worship as the apostles did? If so, this book is for you. It is dynamic in its simplicity and still is.

Do you take for granted that the founders of major Christian denominations would approve of the way your denomination worships today? Find numerous quotes from them at the beginning of each chapter on various forms of worship we engage in.

Do you take for granted that second-century apostolic fathers worshiped the same way your congregation worships today? You will find at the end of each chapter quotations from these early Christian leaders in the 2nd and 3rd centuries about what they approved of and did not approve of in Christian worship.

Do you take for granted that the way your congregation worships is pretty much the same as Christian worship has been since Jesus' apostles began the church? Numerous scriptures are quoted throughout each chapter in order to help the reader know what God wants in worship to him.

This book ends with an appeal that is applicable also to the other book in this two-book series: Can the denominational world unite? Pagan religions and atheism are trying to take hold around the globe, and to choke out Christianity. Divided we fall. United we stand. Let us go forward! Back to the first century.

Thank You

Thanks for reading my book! I'm honored that you chose to spend your precious time with my research. You are appreciated. I'm an independent author who relies on my readers to help spread the word about stories you enjoy. Would you take a few minutes to let your friends know on Facebook, Pinterest... wherever you go online?

Also, each honest review at online retailers means a lot to me and helps other readers know if this is a book they might enjoy,

I welcome contact from readers. At my website (below), you can do so. You can also sign up for my newsletter (below) to be notified of half-price books and new releases.

Buy Your Next Book Now

CHRISTIAN LIFE
Applied Christianity: Handbook 500 Good Works
You Can Be a Hero Alone
Worship Changes Since 1st Century + Worship 1sr Century Way
The Best of Alexander Campbell's Millennial Harbinger
Inside the Hearts of Bible Women-Reader+Audio+Leader
The Lord's Supper: 52 Readings with Prayers
http://bit.ly/Christianlife

BIBLE TEXT STUDIES
Revelation: A Love Letter From God
The Holy Spirit: 592 Verses Examined
Was Jesus God? (Why Evil)
365 Life-Changing Scriptures Day by Date
Love Letters of Jesus & His Bride, Ecclesia
Christianity or Islam? The Contrast
The Road to Heaven
http://bit.ly/BibleTexts

FUN BOOKS
Bible Puzzles, Bible Song Book, Bible Numbers
http://bit.ly/BibleFun

TOUCHING GOD SERIES
365 Golden Bible Thoughts: God's Heart to Yours
365 Pearls of Wisdom: God's Soul to Yours
365 Silver-Winged Prayers: Your Spirit to God's
http://bit.ly/TouchingGodSeries

-SURVEY SERIES: EASY BIBLE WORKBOOKS
→Old Testament & New Testament Surveys
→Questions You Have Asked-Part I & II
http://bit.ly/BibleWorkbooks

HISTORICAL RESEARCH BIBLE
for Novel, Screenwriter, Documentary & Thesis Writers
http://bit.ly/32uZkHa

GENEALOGY: How to Climb Your Family Tree Without Falling Out
Volume I & 2: Beginner-Intermediate & Colonial-Medieval
http://bit.ly/GenealogyBeginner-Advanced

Connect With The Author

Website: https://inspirationsbykatheryn.com

Facebook: bit.ly/FacebooksKatherynMaddoxHaddad

Linkedin: http://bit.ly/KatherynLinkedin

Twitter: https://twitter.com/KatherynHaddad

Pinterest: https://www.pinterest.com/haddad1940/

Goodreads: https://www.goodreads.com/katherynmaddoxhaddad

Get A Free Book
Sign up for Katheryn's monthly newsletter with half-price books for the whole family and insider tips on what's coming next.
http://bit.ly/katheryn

Join My Dream Team
Members get the first peek at my newest book and have fun offering me advice sometimes. I have a point system of rewards for helping me get the word out. Check it out here:
http://bit.ly/KatherynsDreamTeam

www.ingramcontent.com/pod-product-compliance
Lightning Source LLC
Chambersburg PA
CBHW071608080526
44588CB00010B/1066